AF226055

SUMMER

In the Creasey Mahan Nature Preserve

ALSO EXPLORE THESE BOOKS IN THE CREASEY MAHAN COLLECTION

One Foggy Morning in Winter
One Foggy Spring Morning
Spring
One Foggy Morning in Summer

SUMMER

In the Creasey Mahan Nature Preserve

Photography by Karin and Katy Acree

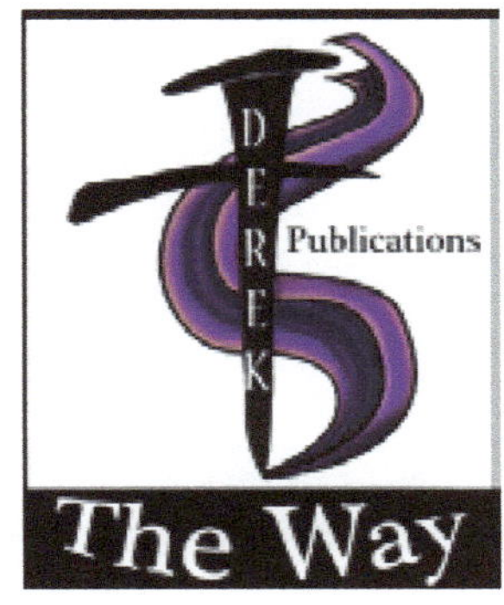

Photographs taken by Karin & Katy Acree

Scripture quotations taken from the ESV® Bible (The Holy Bible, English Standard Version®), copyright © 2001 by Crossway, a publishing ministry of Good News Publishers. Used by permission. All rights reserved.

Scripture quotations taken from the New American Standard Bible ® (NASB) Copyright © 1960, 1962, 1963, 1968, 1971, 1972, 1973, 1975, 1977, 1995 by The Lockman Foundation. Used by permission. www.Lockman.org.

Scripture quotations marked NIV are taken from The *Holy Bible*, *New International Version*® , NIV ® Copyright © 1973, 1978, 1984, 2011 by Biblica, Inc.™ Used by permission of Zondervan.

Scripture taken from the New King James Version®. Copyright © 1982 by Thomas Nelson. Used by permission. All rights reserved.

Scripture quotations marked NLT are taken from the *Holy Bible*, New Living Translation, copyright© 1996, 2004, 2015 by Tyndale House Foundation. Used by permission of Tyndale House Publishers, Inc., Carol Stream, Illinois 60188. All rights reserved.

Printed in the United States of America

ISBN: 978-1-937979-36-2

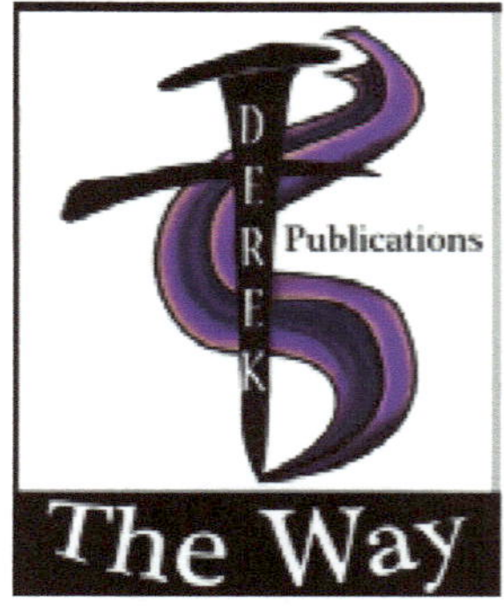

Goshen, KY 40026
www.derekpublications.com

DEDICATION

To Debbie

Happy Birthday!

FORWARD
About the Creasey Mahan Collection

Karin's books represent well the words of poet and philosopher, Henry David Thoreau: "Heaven is under our feet as well as over our heads." Each photograph in this series captures a cherished moment – raindrops that look like jewels, a lightning bug as it rests on a leaf, sunlight streaming through trees and a Red-tailed Hawk soaring overhead. Her images are like prayers that remind us to slow down, enjoy each moment and behold every blessing that may appear before us.

When Karin first showed me her photographs and the accompanying passages contained in this series of scripture books, I was in awe of her talent, dedication and the many hours she spent alone and with her daughters, as they walked the scenic trails at Creasey Mahan Nature Preserve. The quotes that accompany the photographs match each image perfectly.

My hope is that you, the reader, will take time to let each image and scripture wash over you. Karin's books invite us to walk alongside her as she notices that "He has made everything beautiful in its time." (Ecclesiastes 3:11)

continued...

Creasey Mahan Nature Preserve is a public charity that serves nearly 50,000 visitors each year. Visitors may enjoy 170 acres of rolling hills, open grasslands, year-round streams, nine-miles of trails and a two-acre woodland garden. Families appreciate the annual events, Thrive Forest School programs, Forest Friends Playground and the Nature Center. Creasey Mahan is open 365 days a year from dawn to dusk.

By Tavia Cathcart Brown
Executive Director of Creasey Mahan Nature Preserve

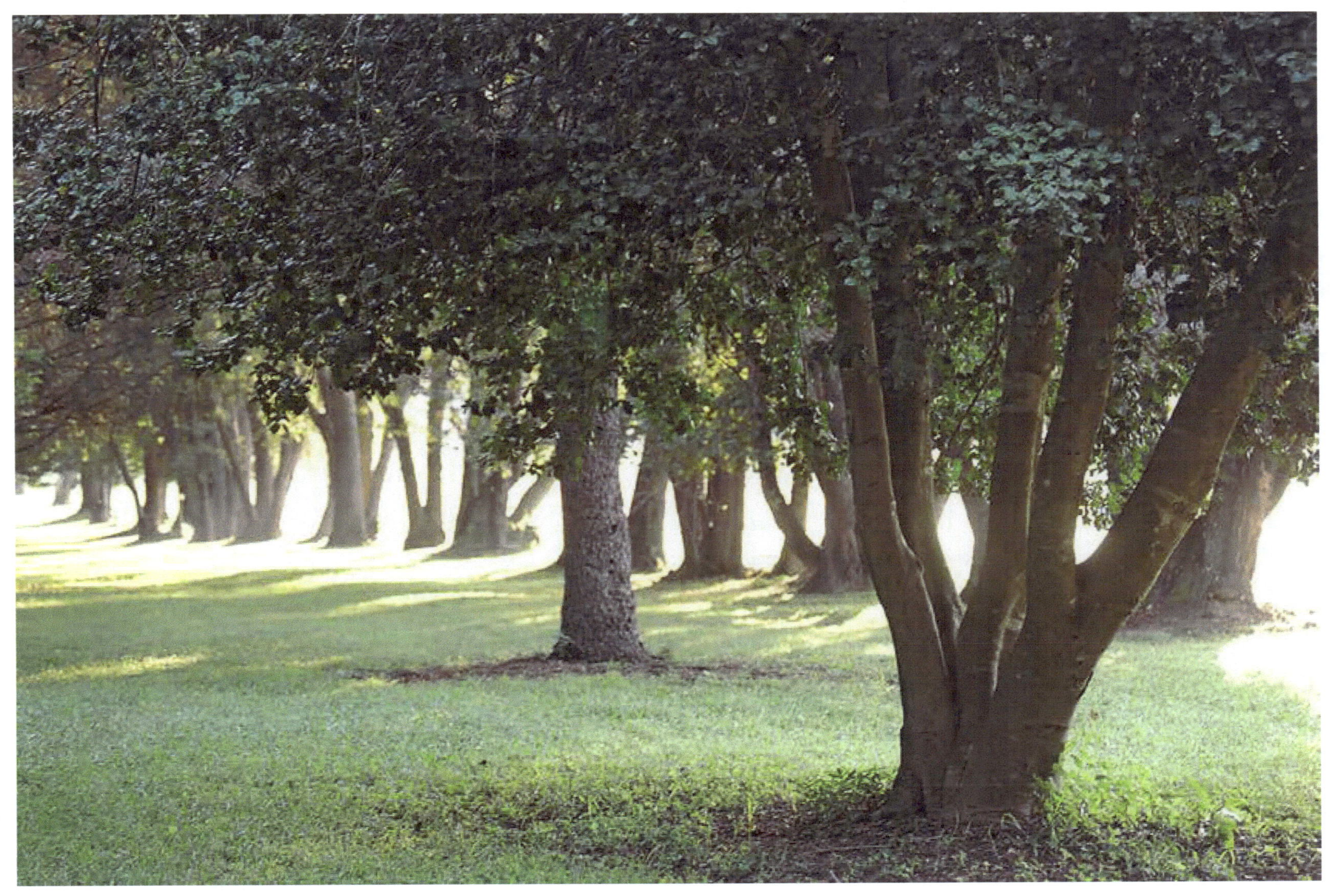

This is the message we have heard from Him and announce to you, that God is Light, and in Him there is no darkness at all.
1 John 1:5-7 (NASB)

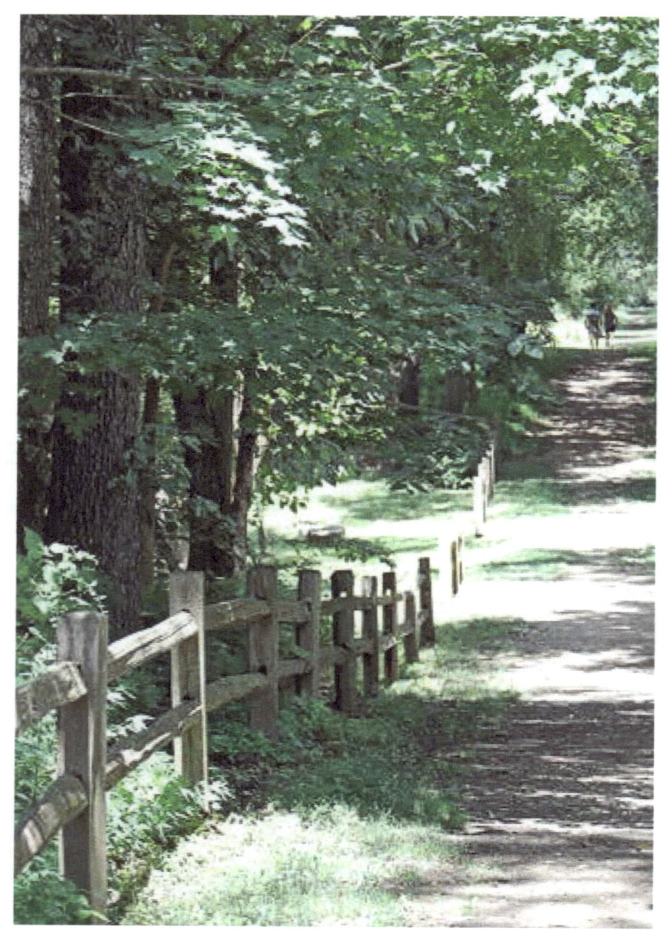
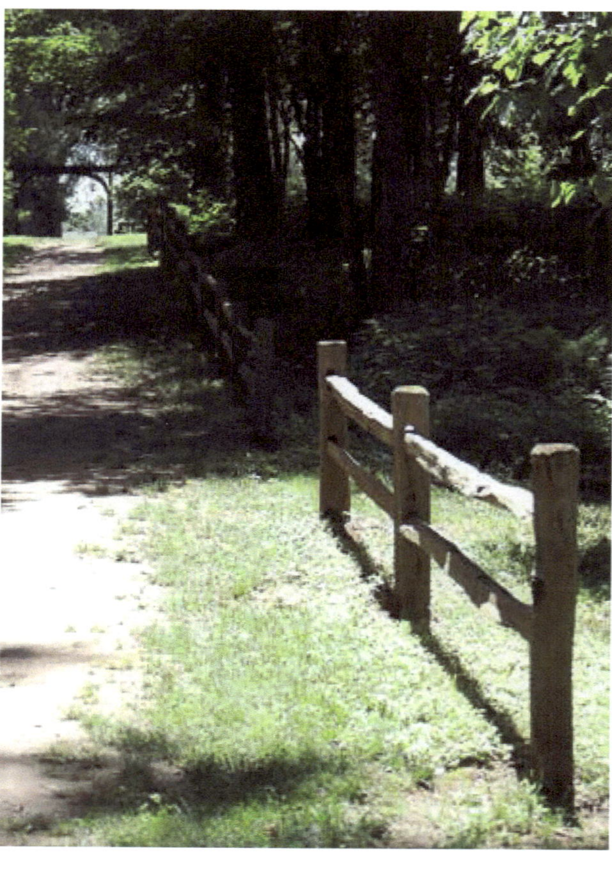
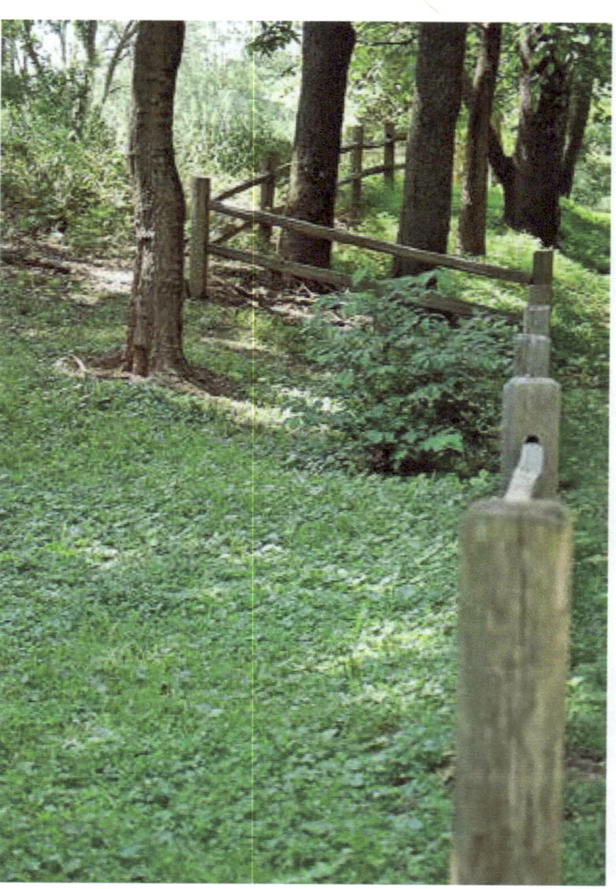

For he himself is our peace,
who has made the two groups one and has destroyed the barrier,
the dividing wall of hostility.
EPHESIANS 2:14 (NIV)

Since God chose to you to be the holy people he loves, you must clothe yourselves with tenderhearted mercy, kindness, humility, gentleness, and patience.
COLOSSIANS 3:12 (NLT)

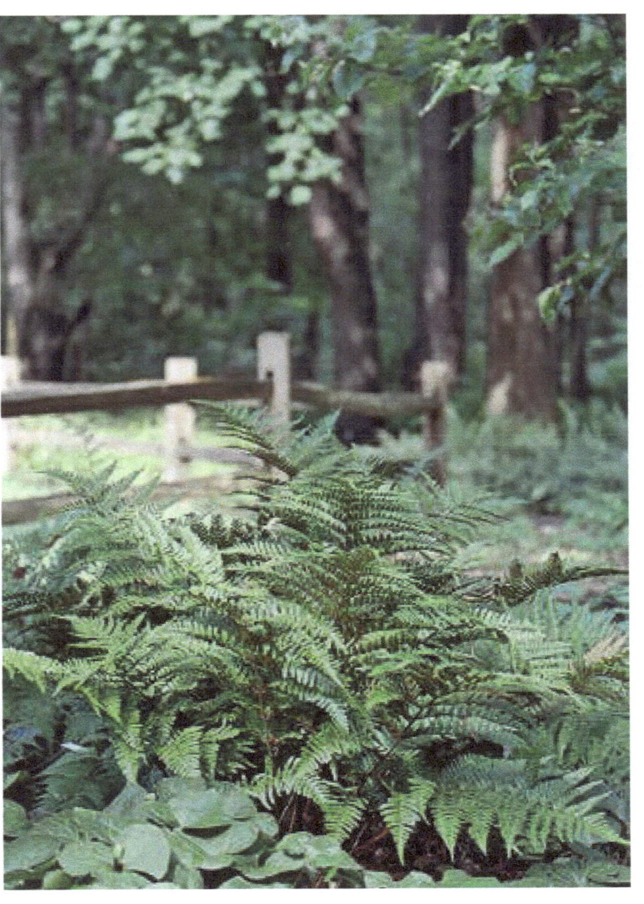

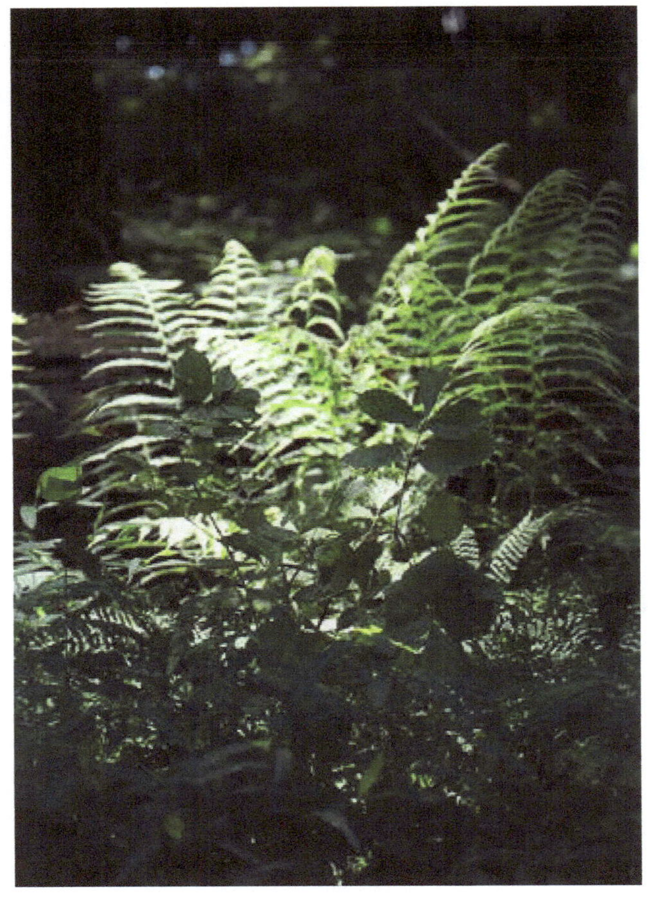

Humble yourselves in the presence of the LORD, and He will exalt you.
JAMES 4:10 (NASB)

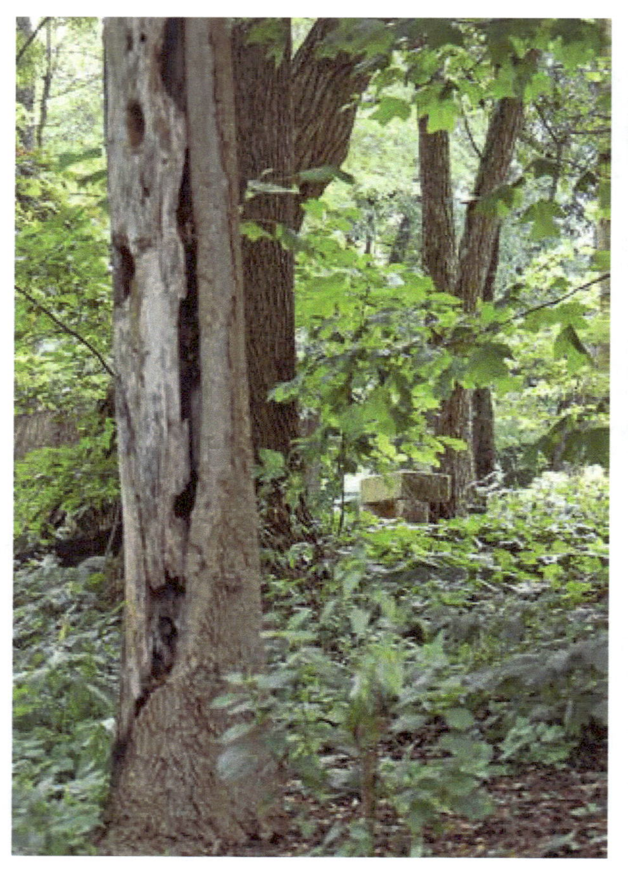
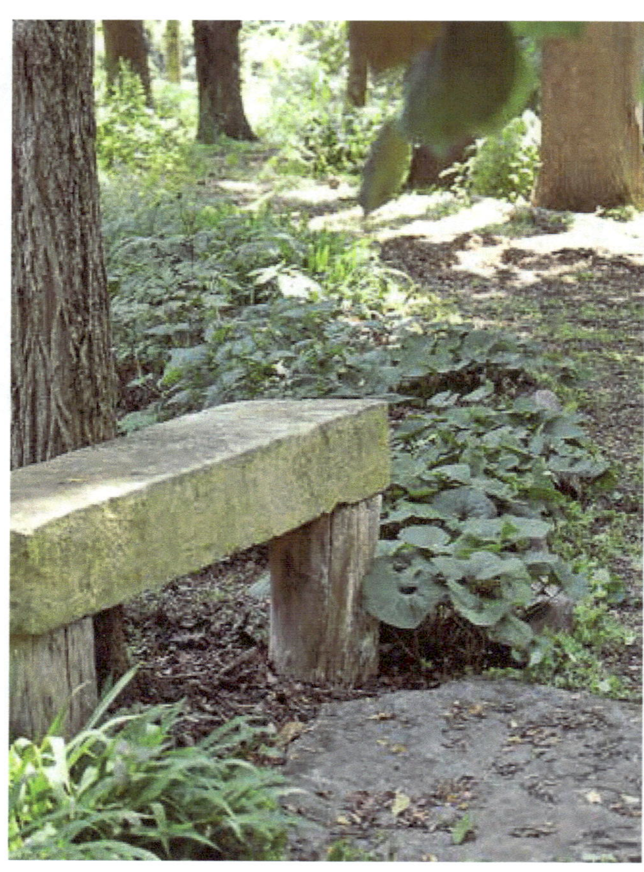
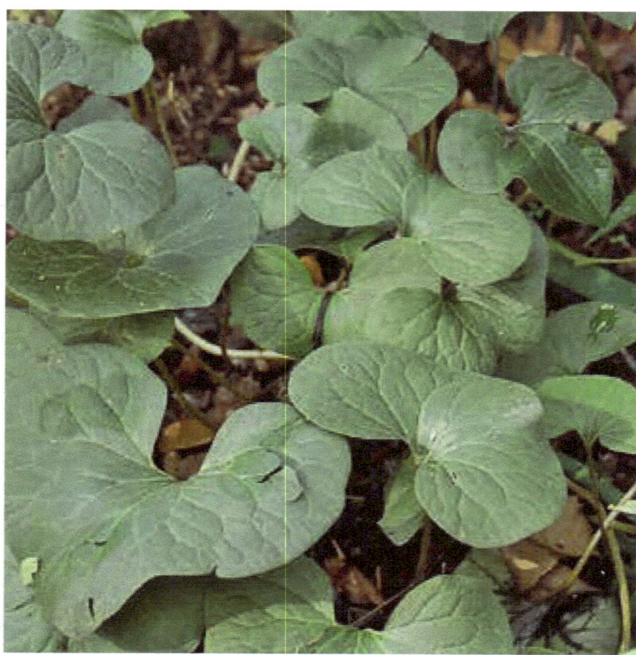

Delight yourself in the LORD,
and he will give you the desires of your heart.
PSALM 37:4 (ESV)

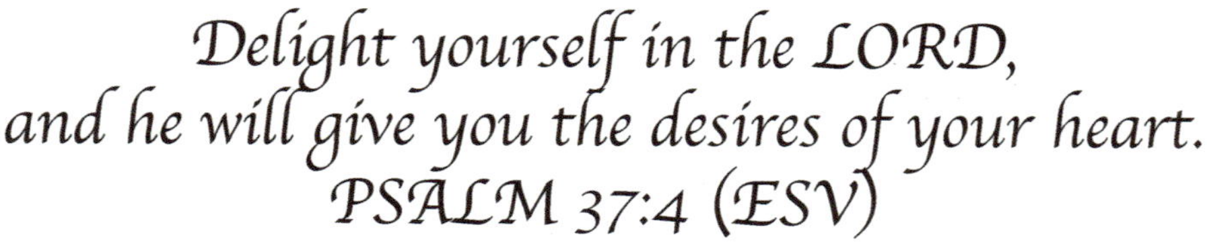
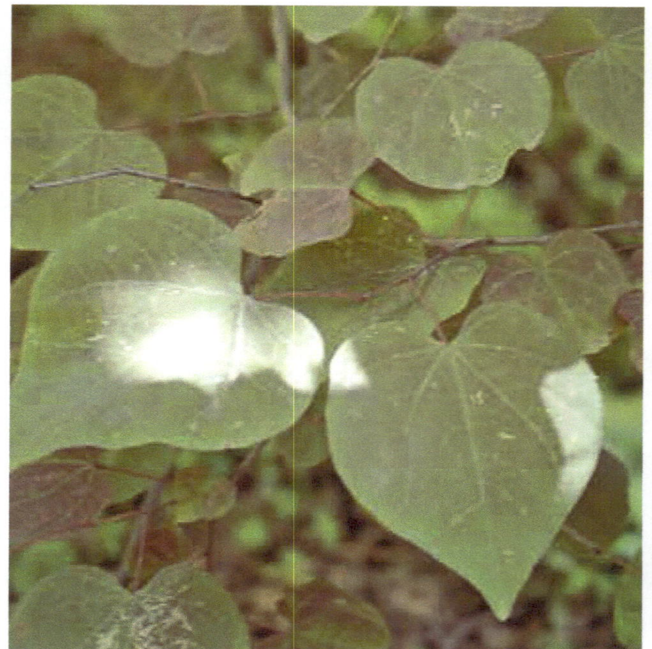

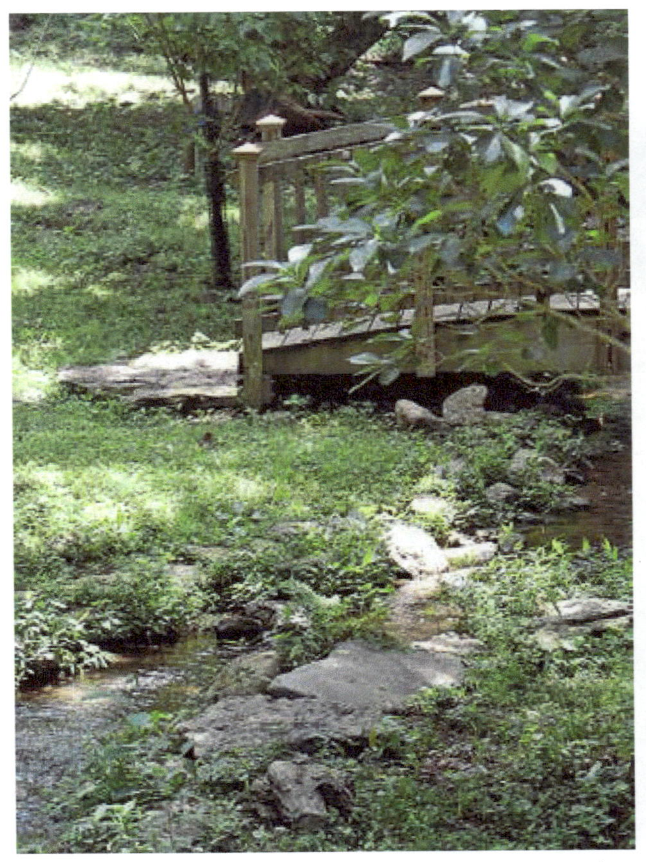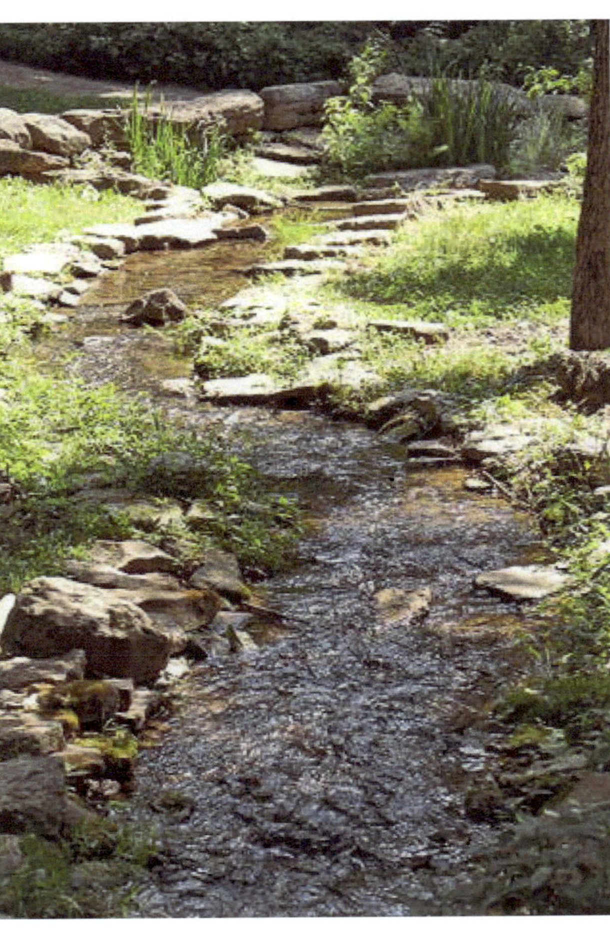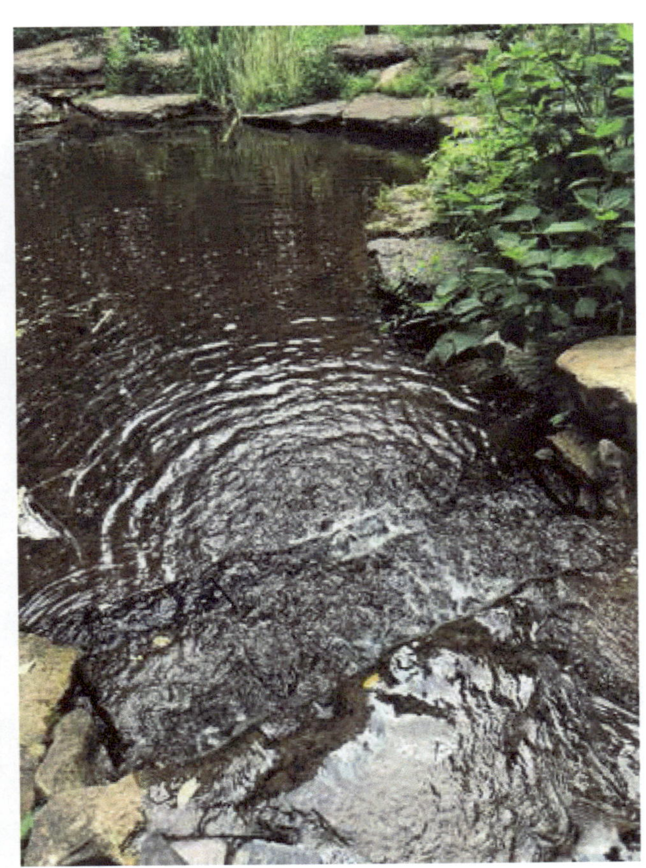

And He said to me, "It is done! I am the Alpha and the Omega,
the Beginning and the End.
To the thirsty I will give of the fountain of the water of life
freely to him who thirsts.
REVELATION 21:6 (NKJV)

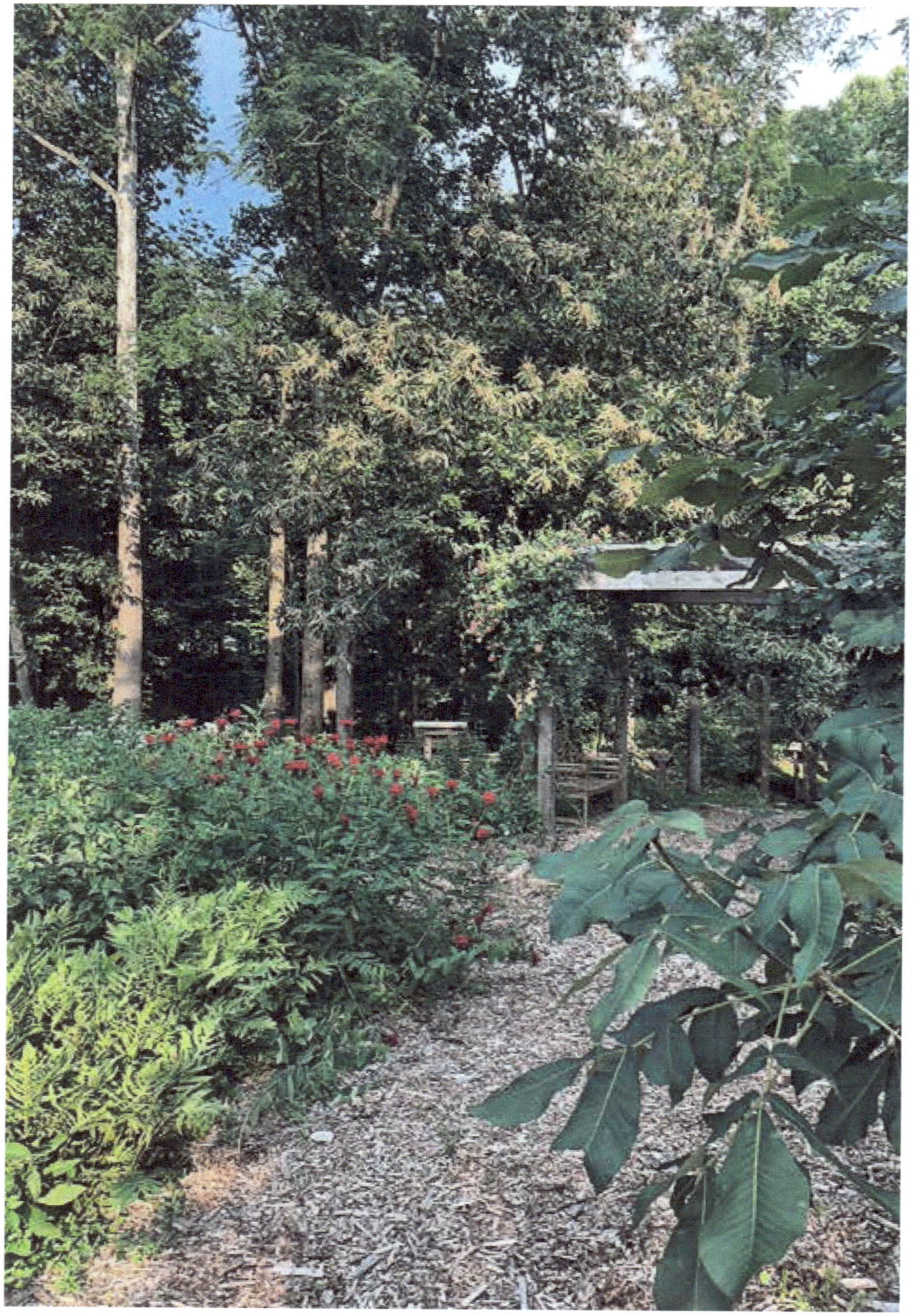

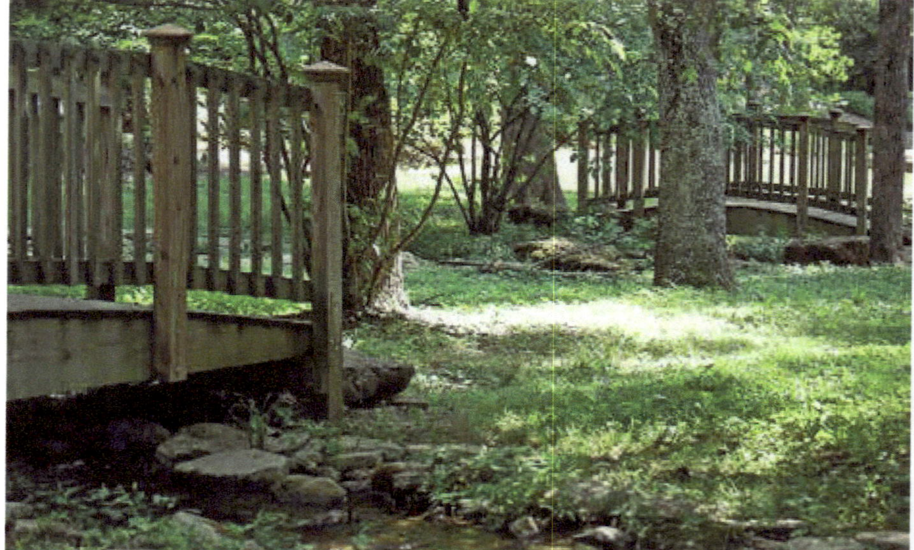

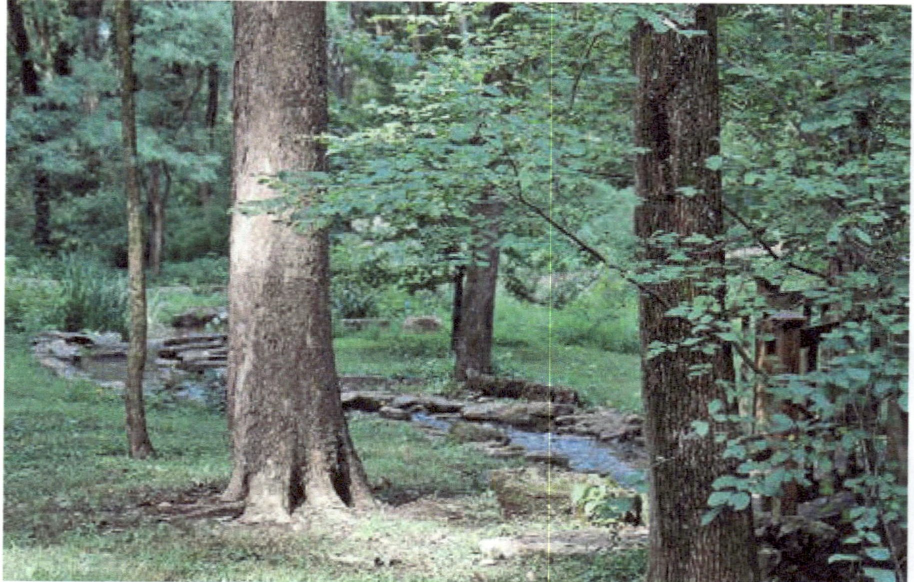

When you turn to the right or to the left, your
ears will hear a voice behind you, saying,
"This is the way; walk in it."
ISAIAH 30:21(NIV)

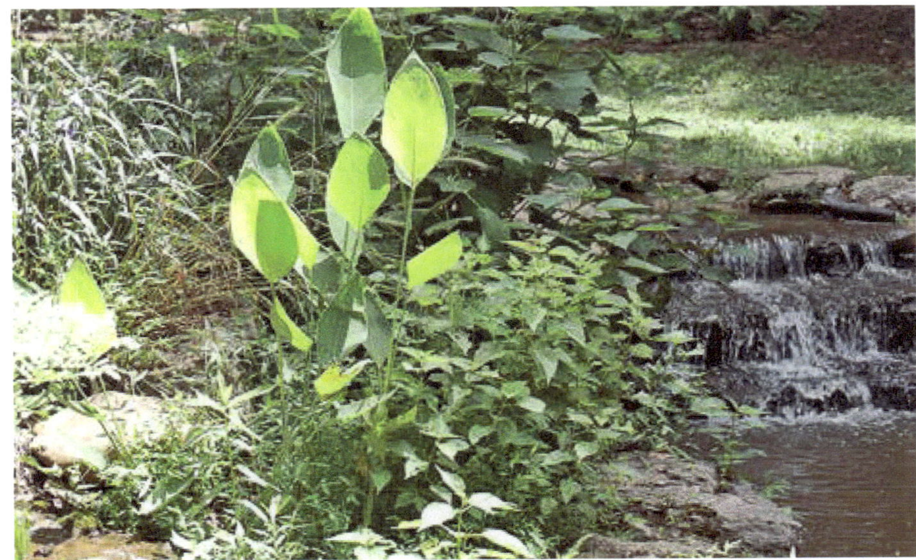

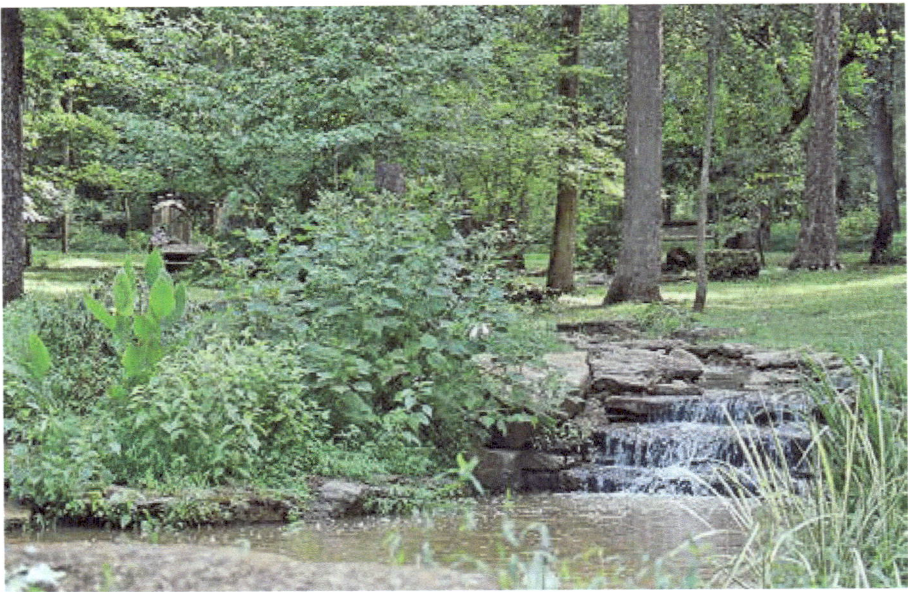

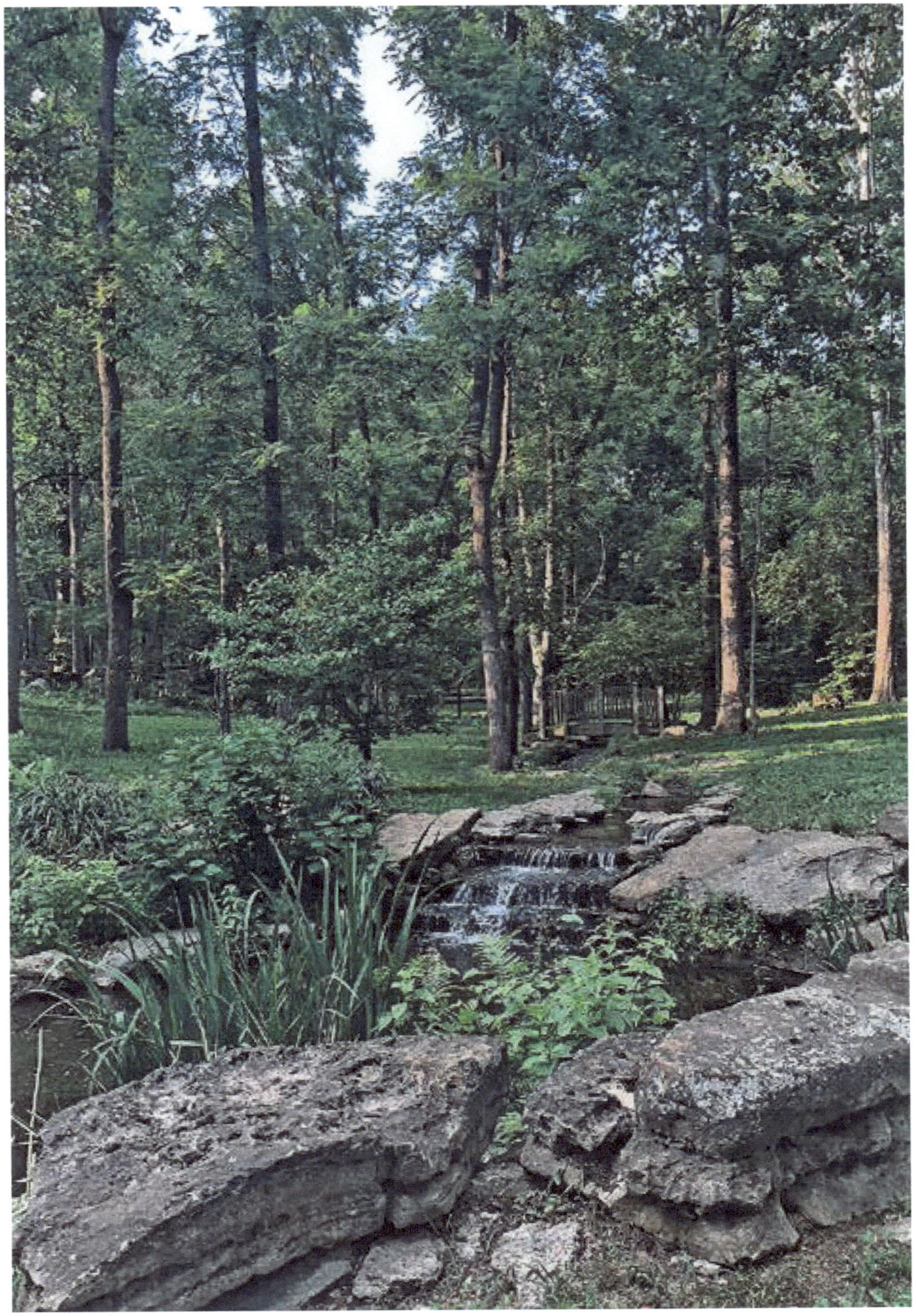

Wise words are like deep waters;
wisdom flows from the wise like a bubbling
brook. PROVERBS 18:4 (NLT)

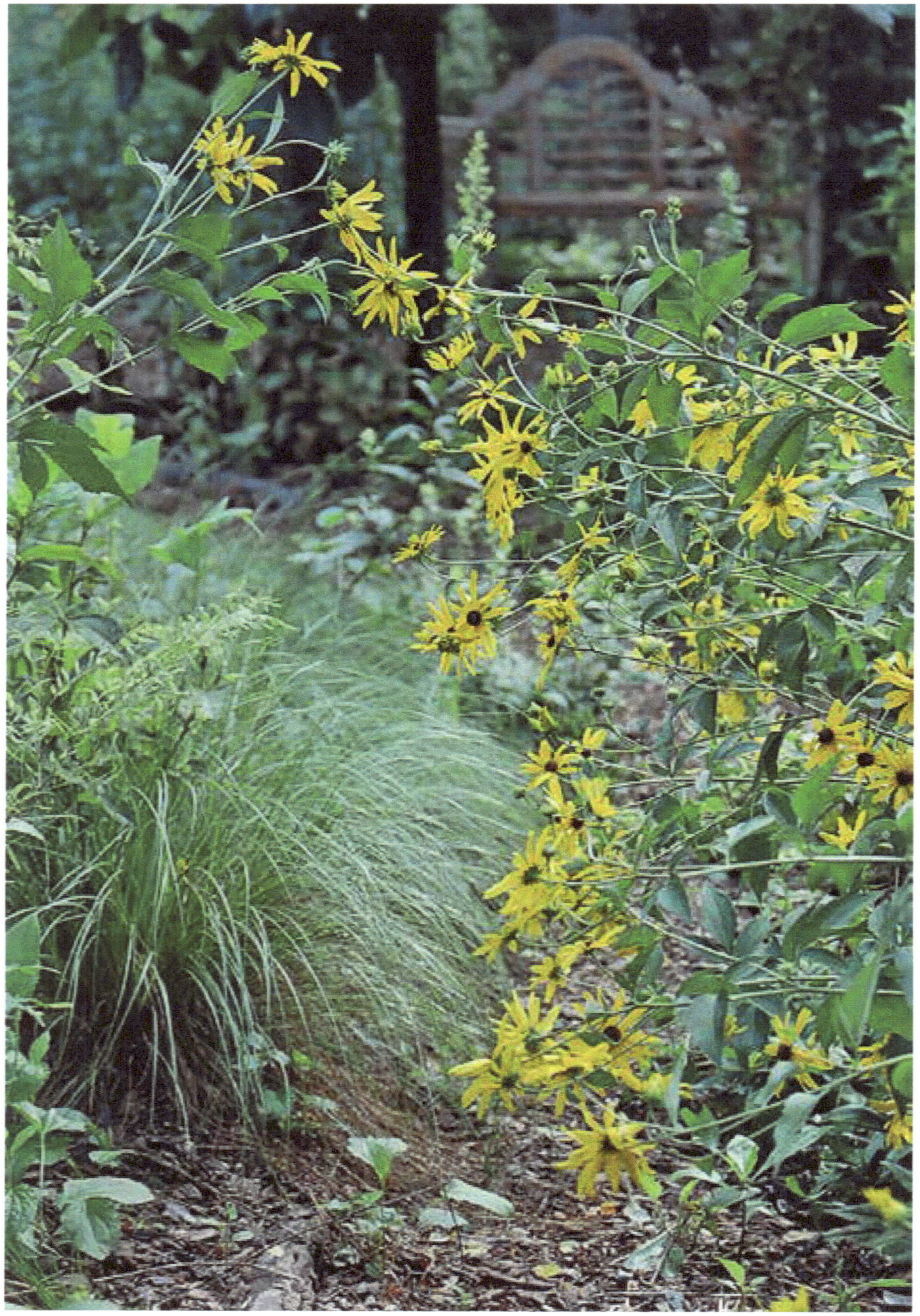

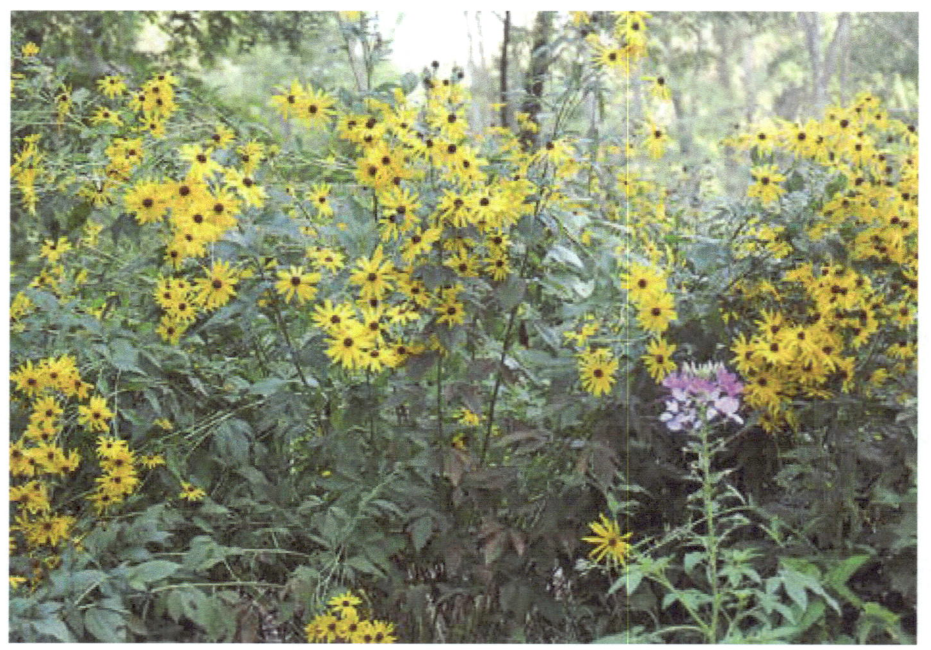

And one called out to another and said,
"Holy, holy, holy is the LORD of hosts, the
whole earth is full of His glory."
ISAIAH 6:3 (NASB)

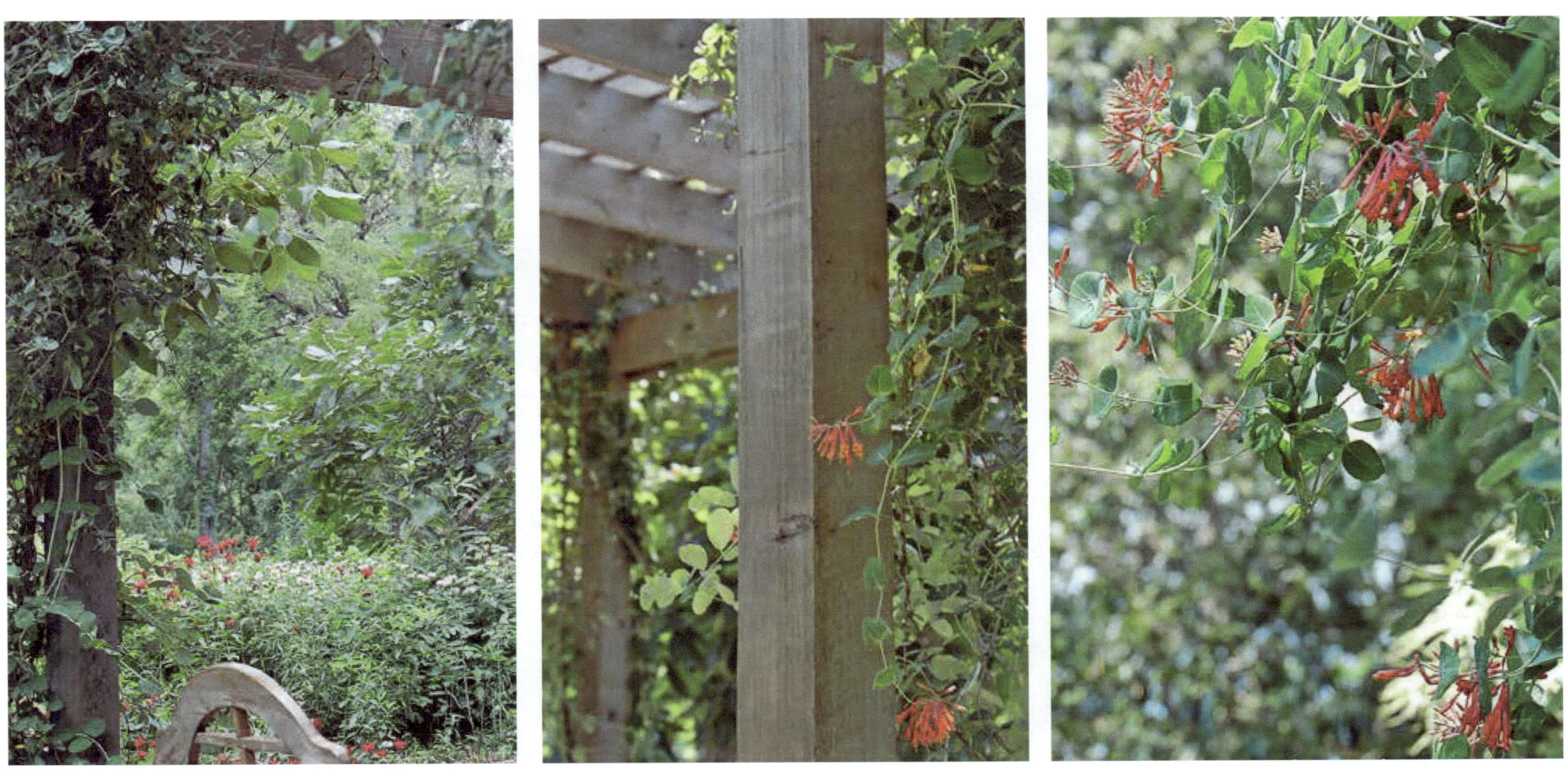

And he will send angels with a loud trumpet call,
and they will gather his elect from the four winds,
from one end of the heavens to the other.
MATTHEW 24:31 (NIV)

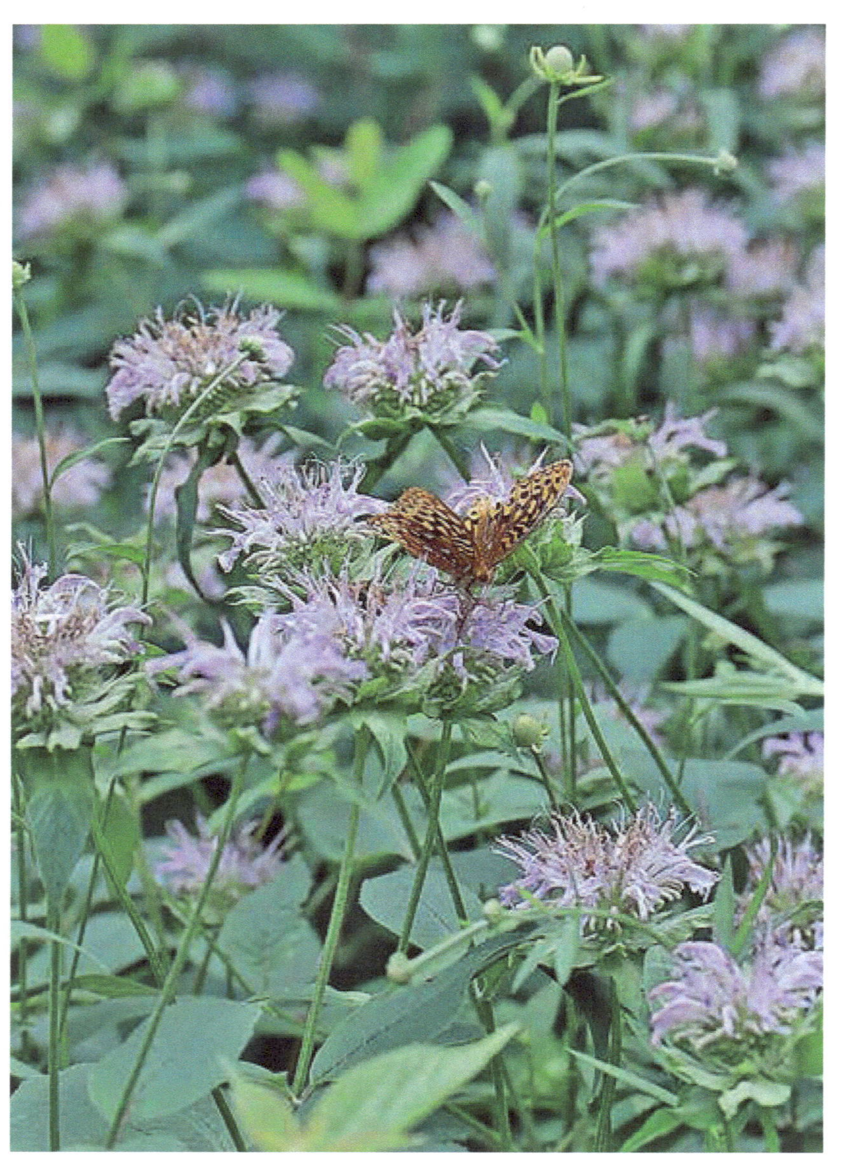

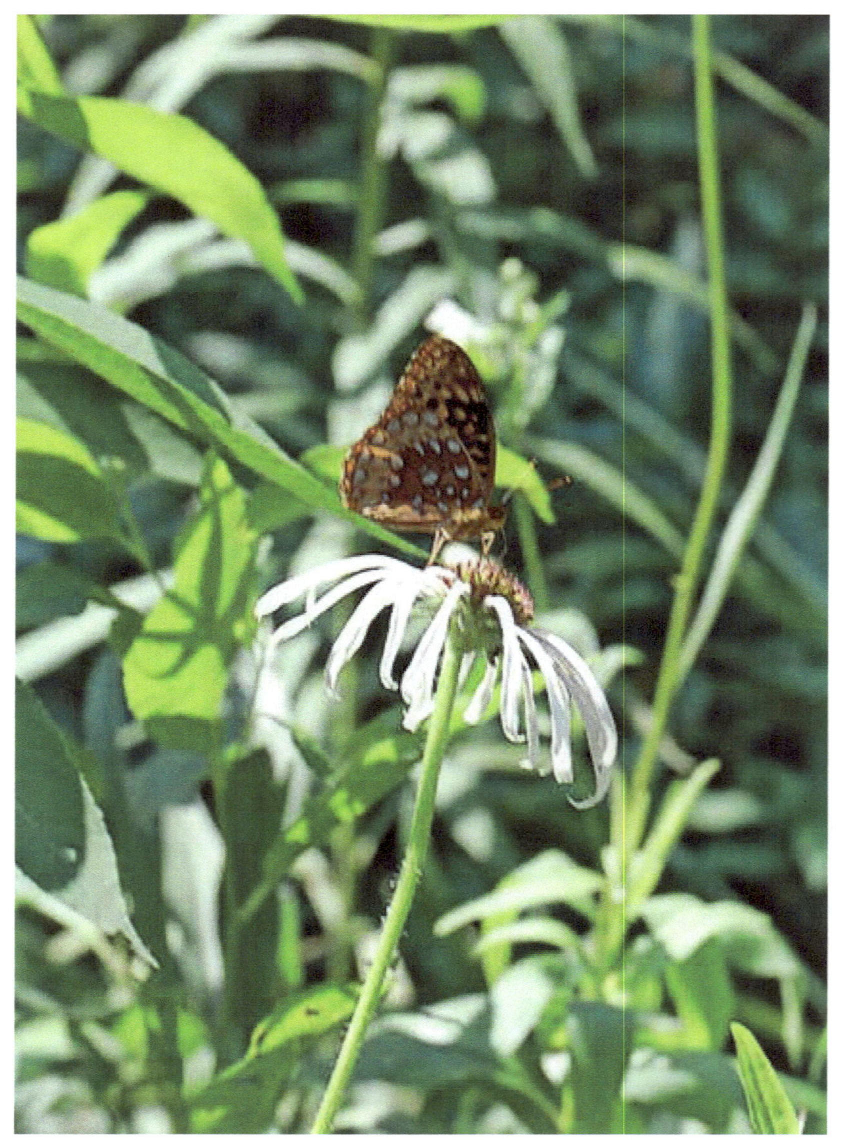

for you have been my help,
and in the shadow of your wings I will sing for joy.
PSALM 63:7 (ESV)

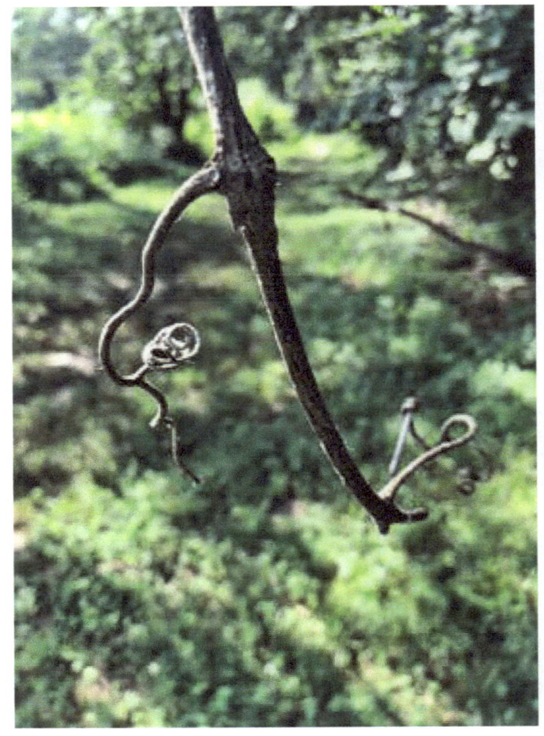
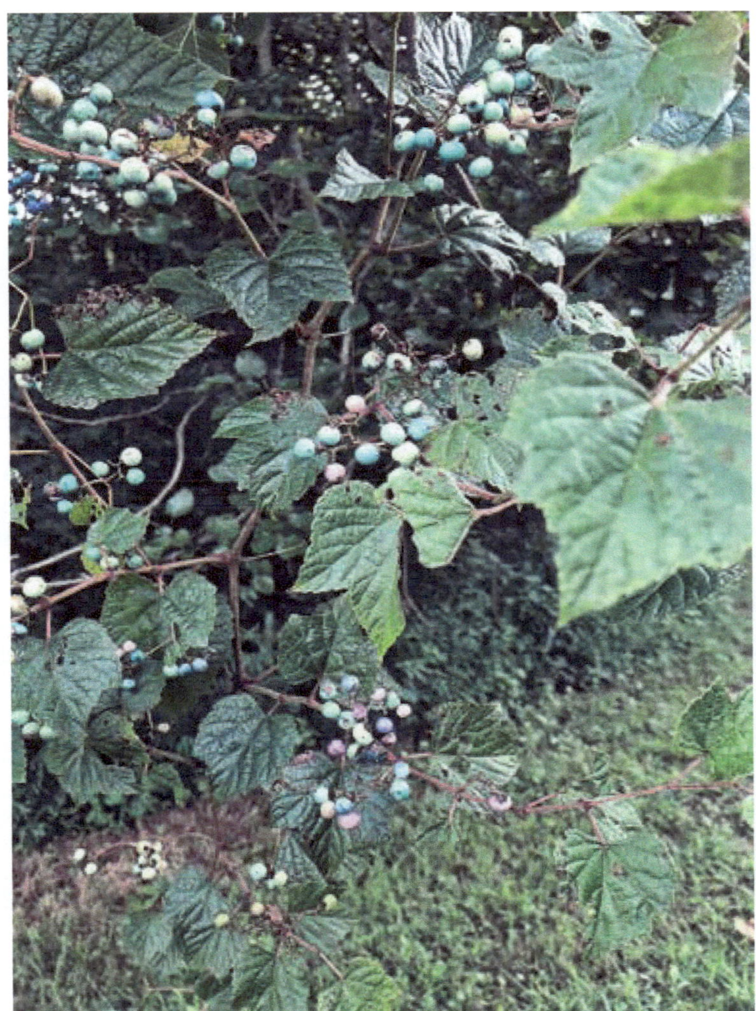
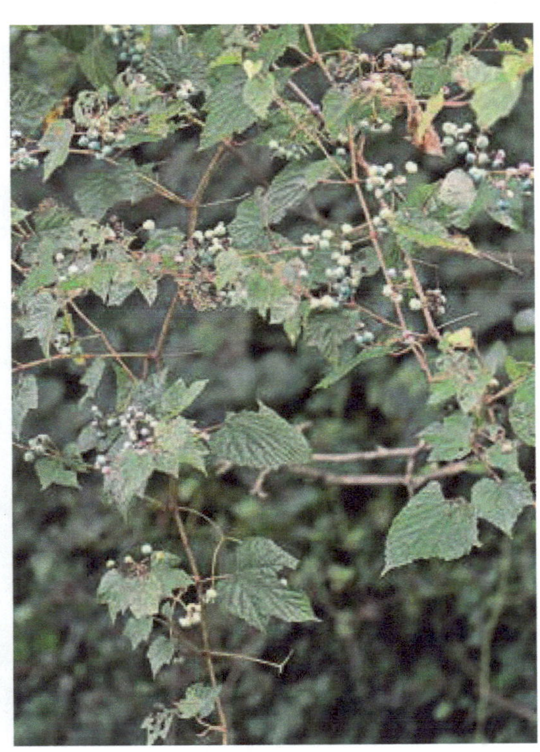

I am the vine, you are the branches;
he who abides in Me and I in him, he bears much fruit,
for apart from Me you can do nothing.
JOHN 15:5 (NASB)

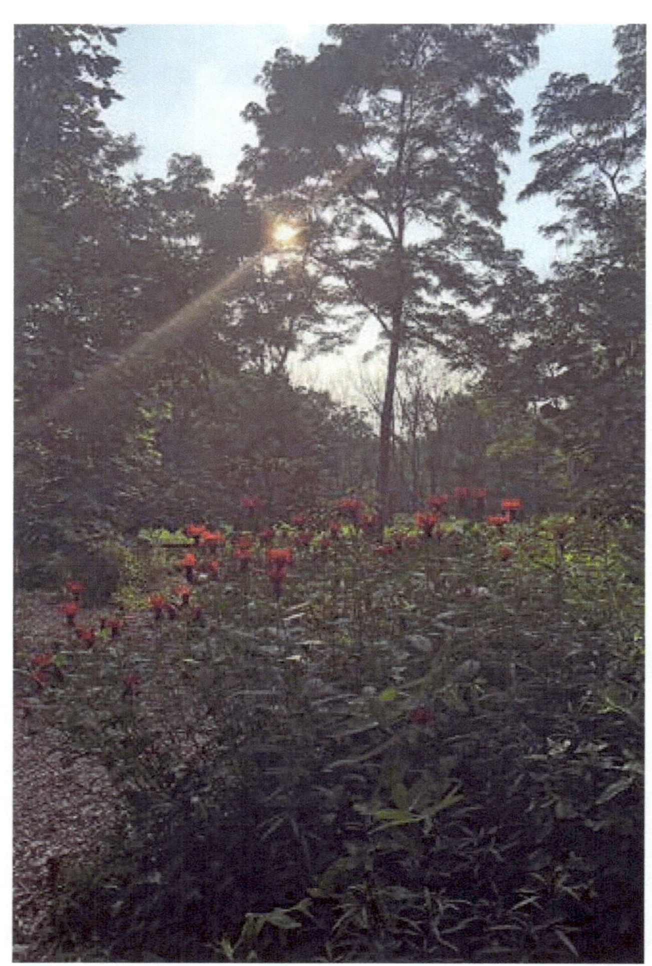
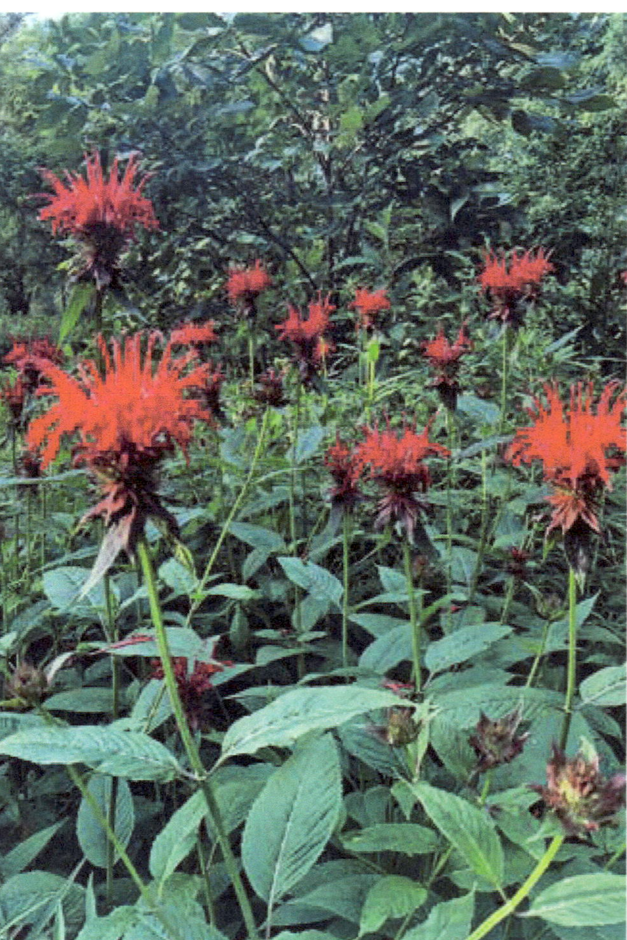
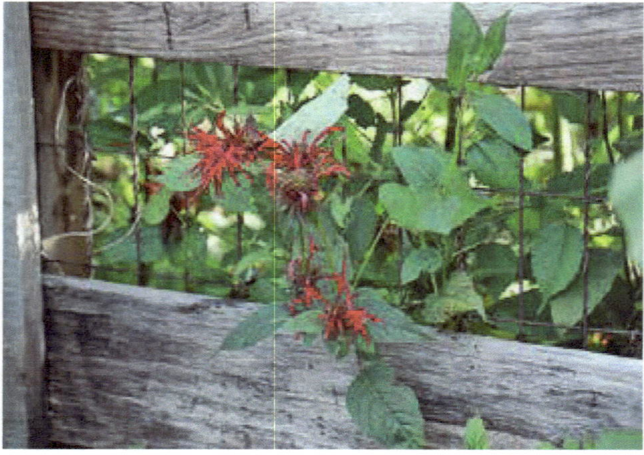
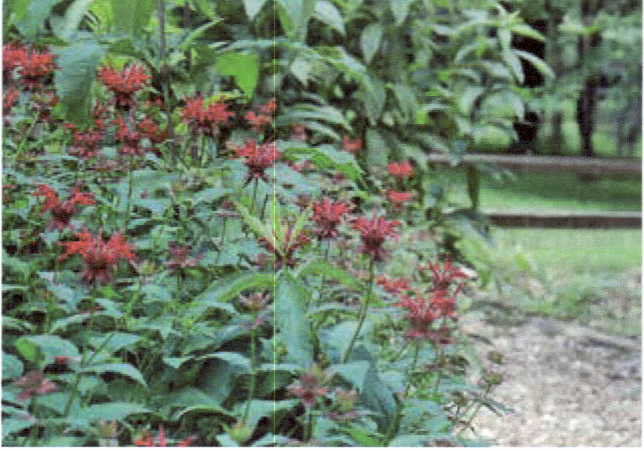

Those that be planted in the house of the LORD shall flourish in the courts of our God.
PSALM 92:13 (NIT)

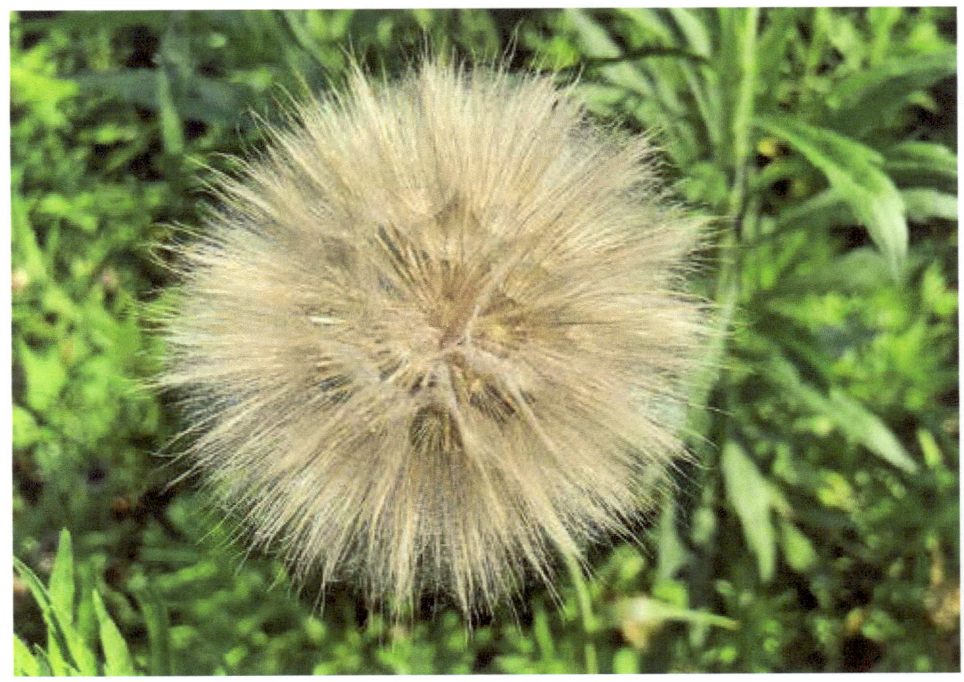

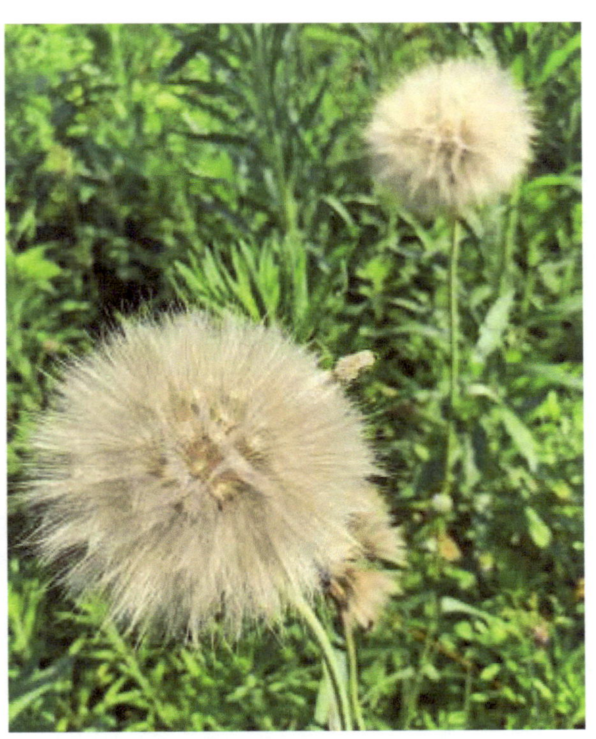

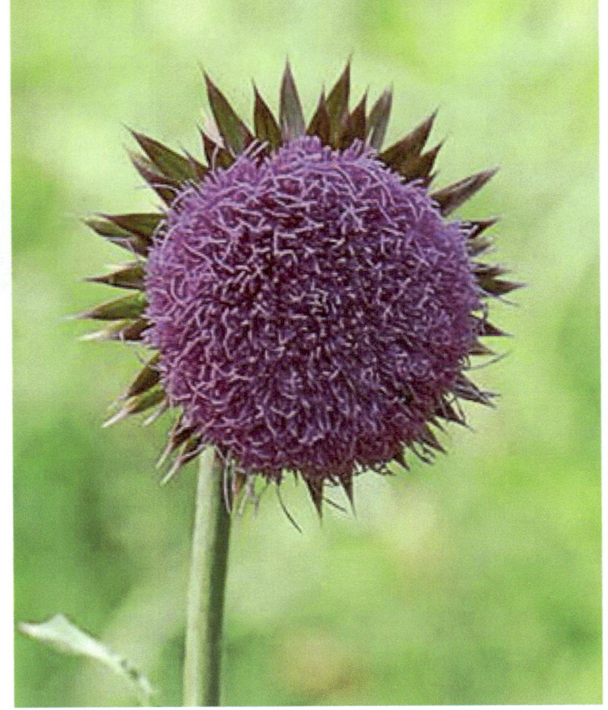

It is He who sits above the circle of the earth...
ISAIAH 40:22 (NKJV)

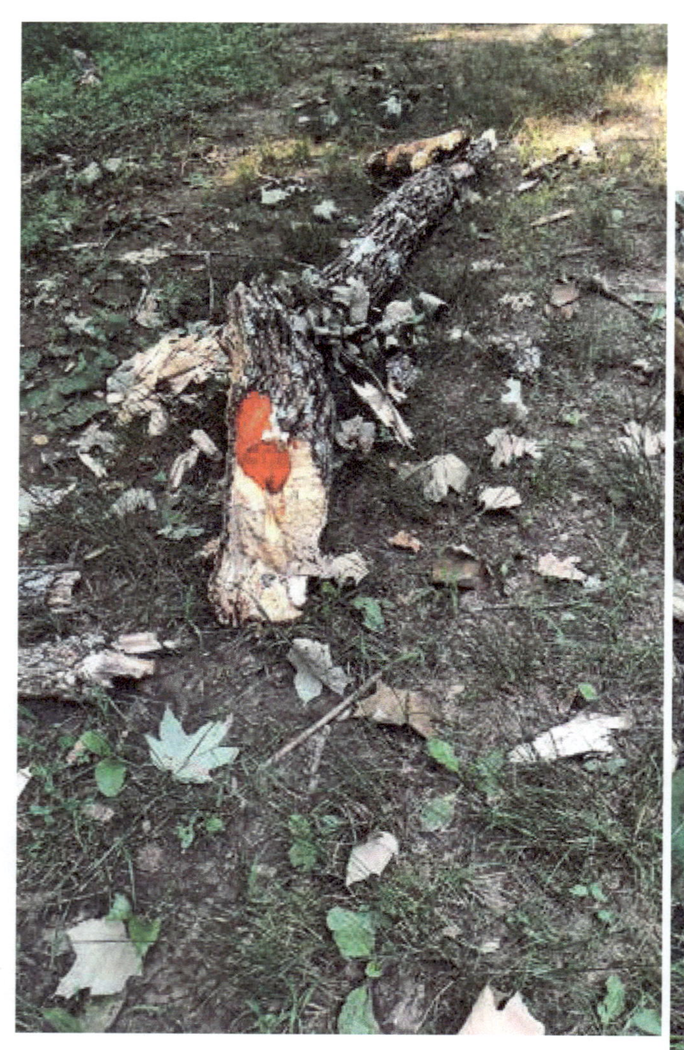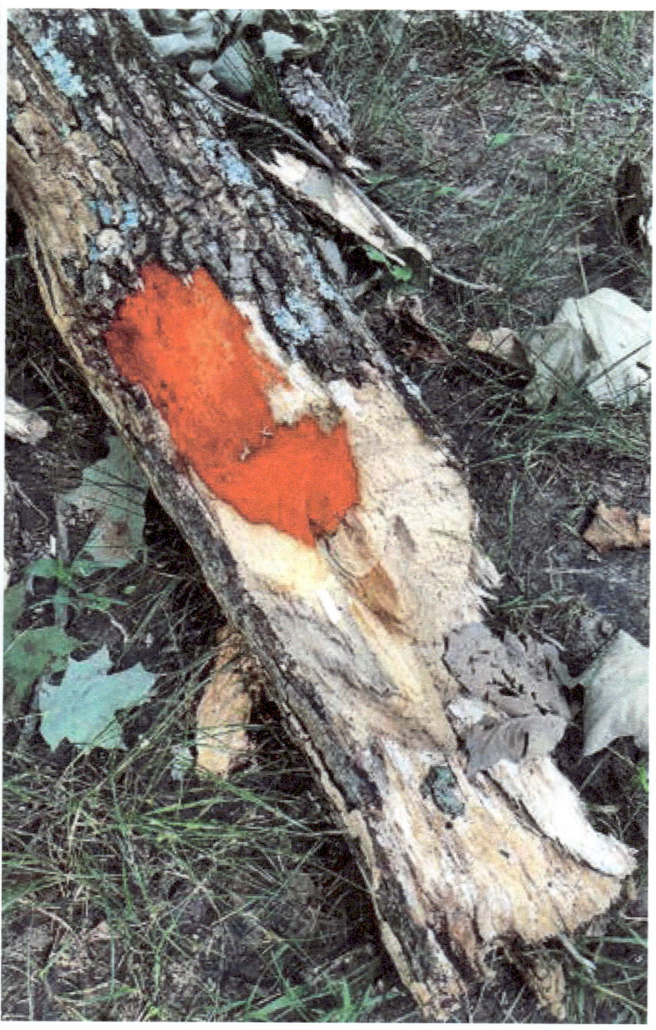

In Him we have
redemption through His blood,
the forgiveness of sins,
according to the riches
of His grace.
EPHESIANS 1:7 (NKJV)

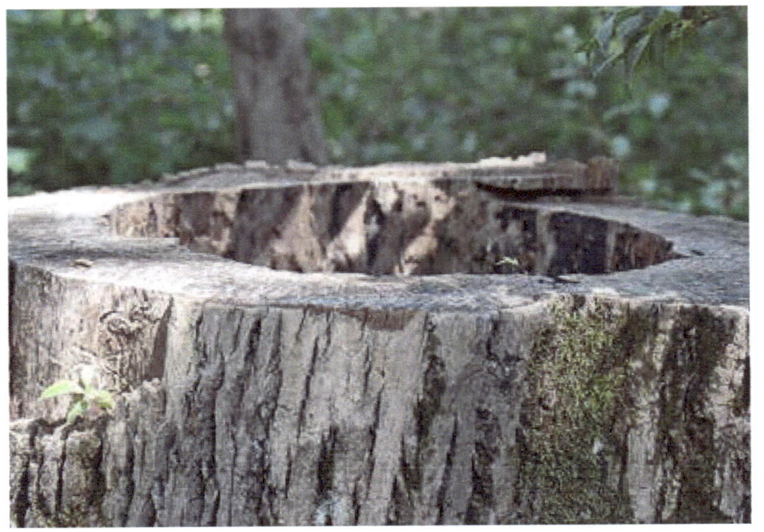

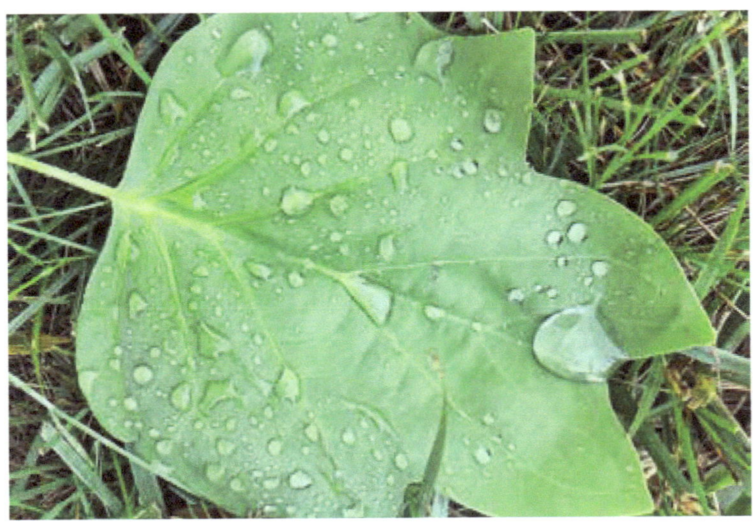

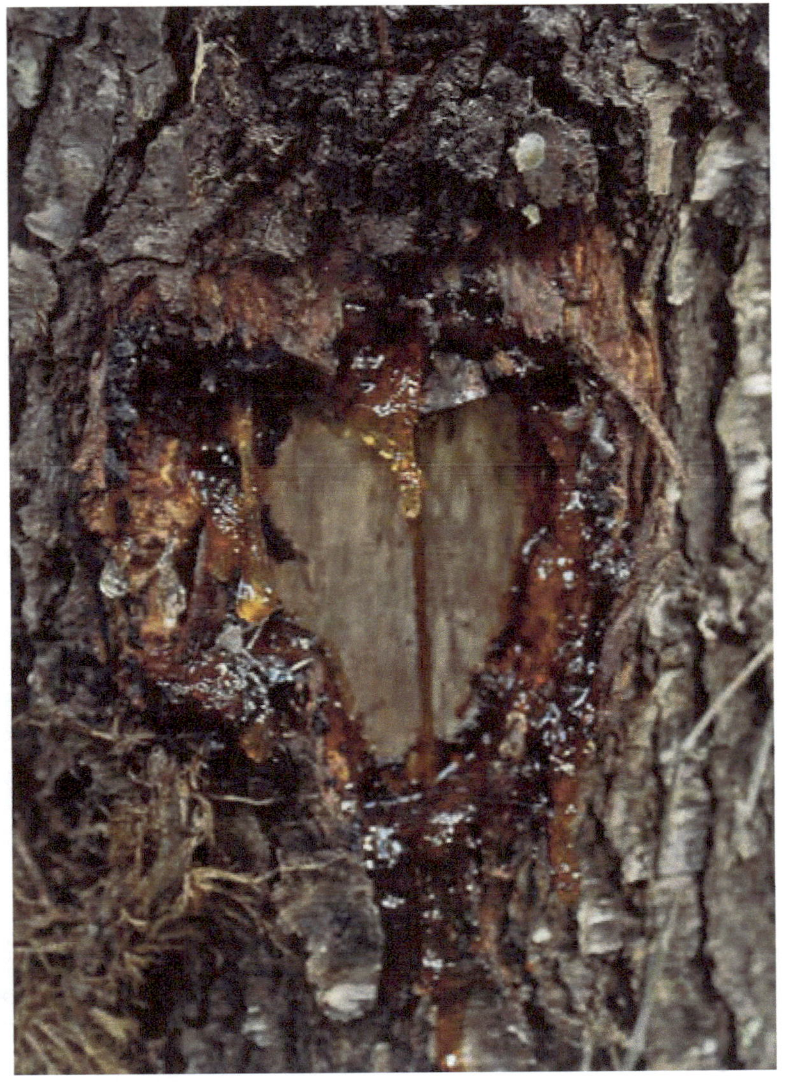

For I wrote you out of great distress and anguish, with a troubled heart and many tears.
I didn't want to grieve you, but I wanted to let you know how much love I have for you.
2 CORINTHIANS 2:4 (NLT)

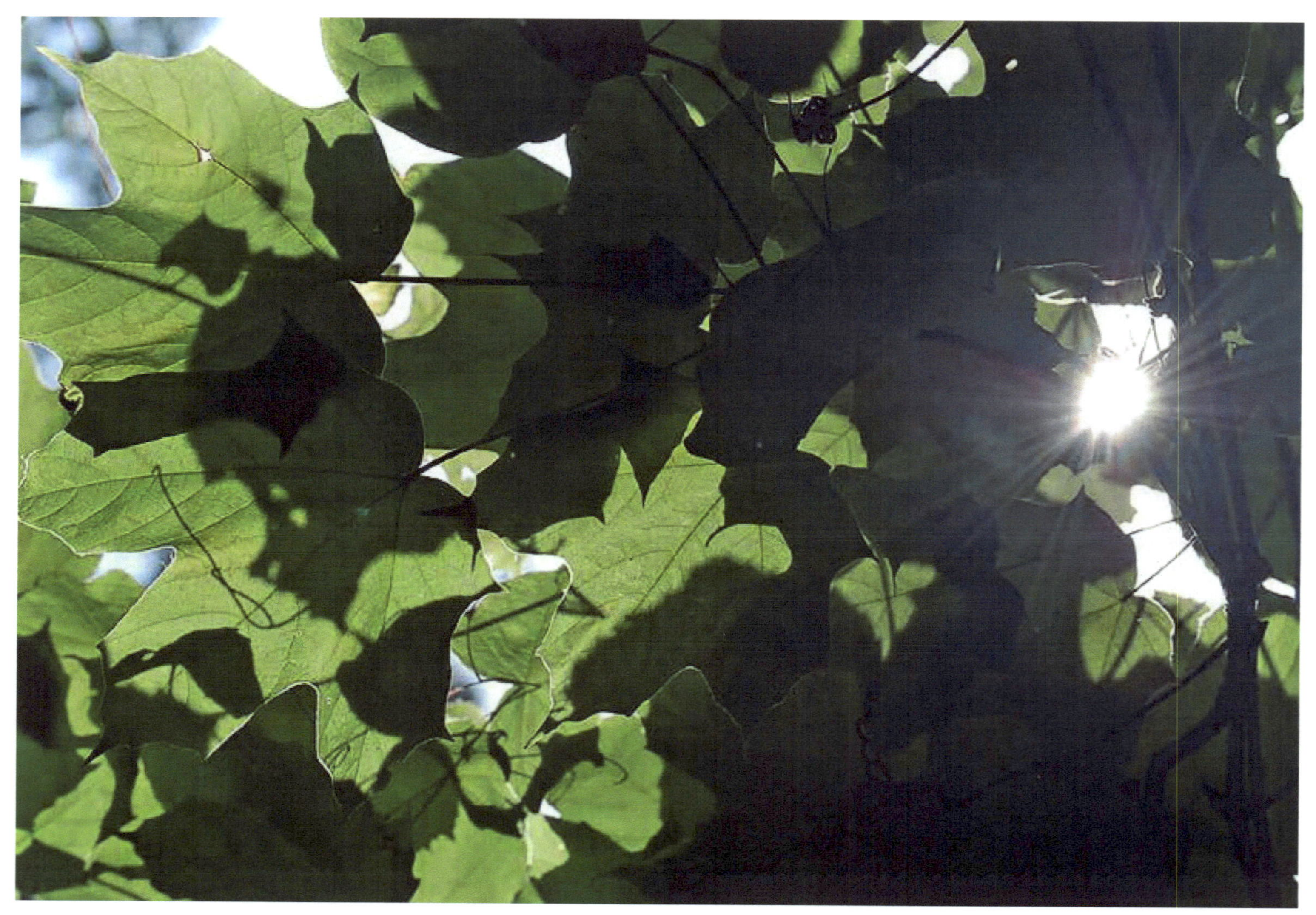

For the LORD God is a sun and shield;
the LORD bestows favor and honor.
No good thing does he withhold from those who walk uprightly.
PSALM 84:11 (ESV)

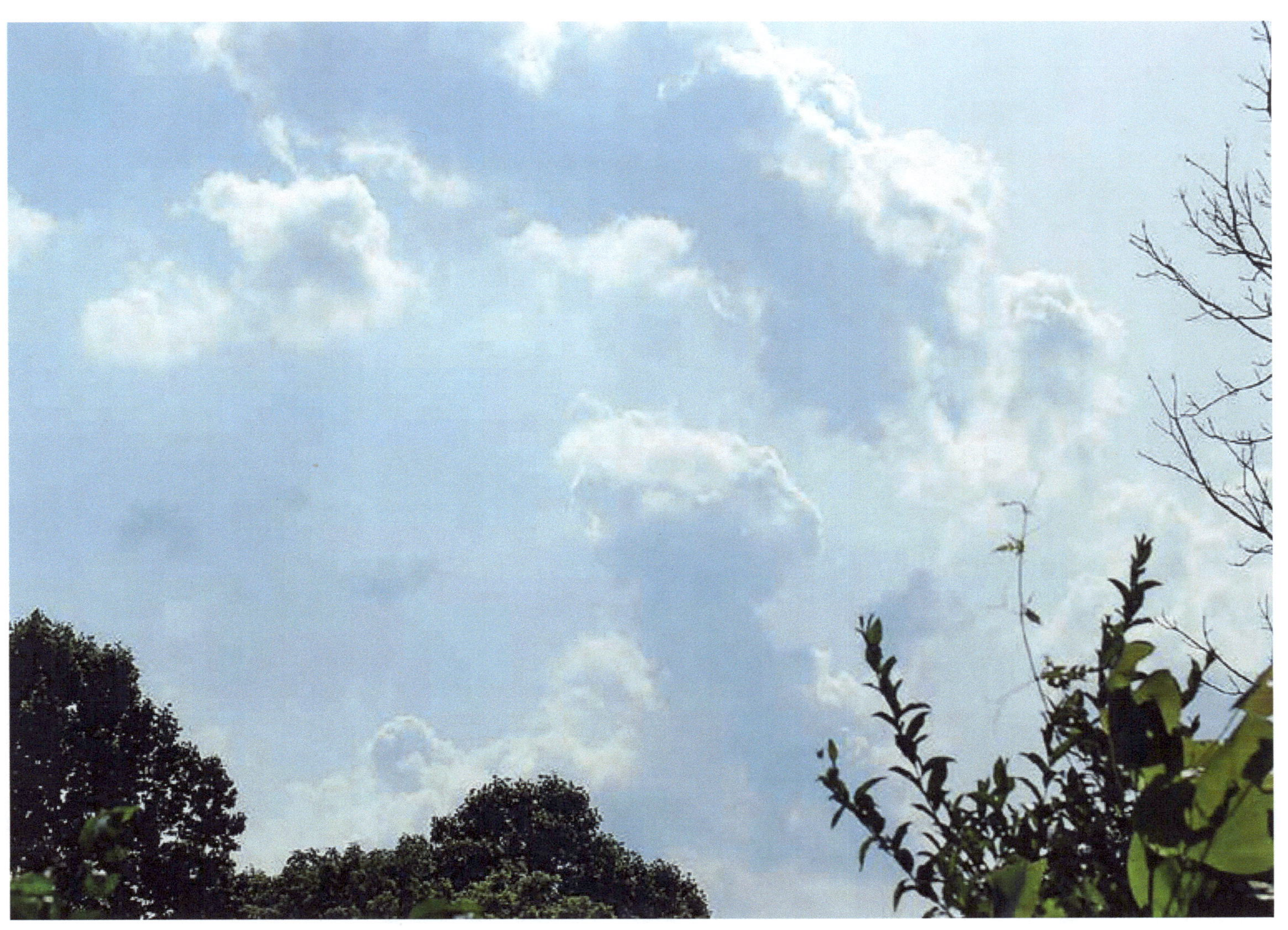

*Do you know how God controls the storm
and causes the lightning to flash from his clouds?
Do you understand how he moves the clouds
with wonderful perfection and skill?
JOB 37: 15-16 (NLT)*

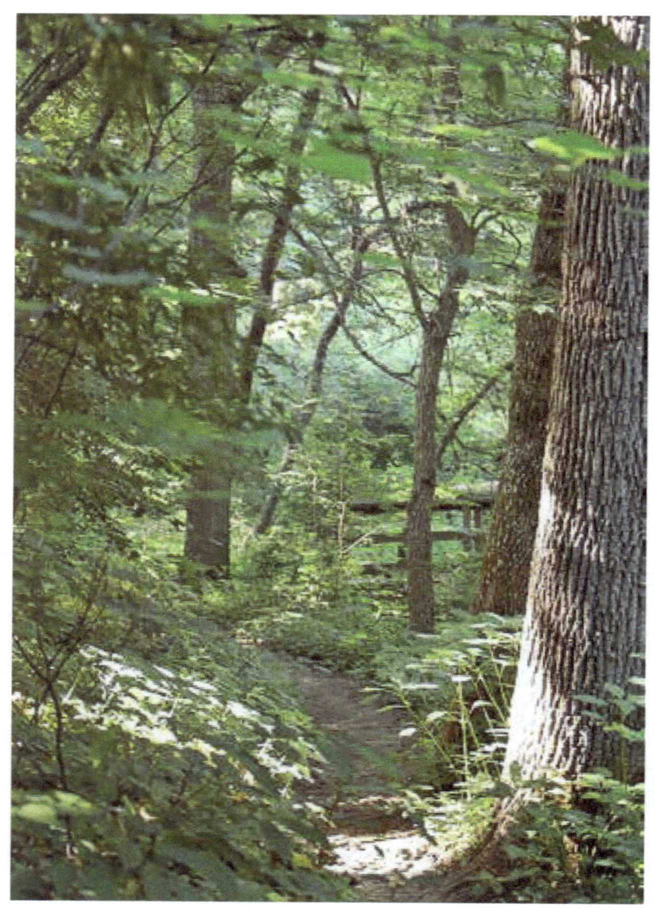 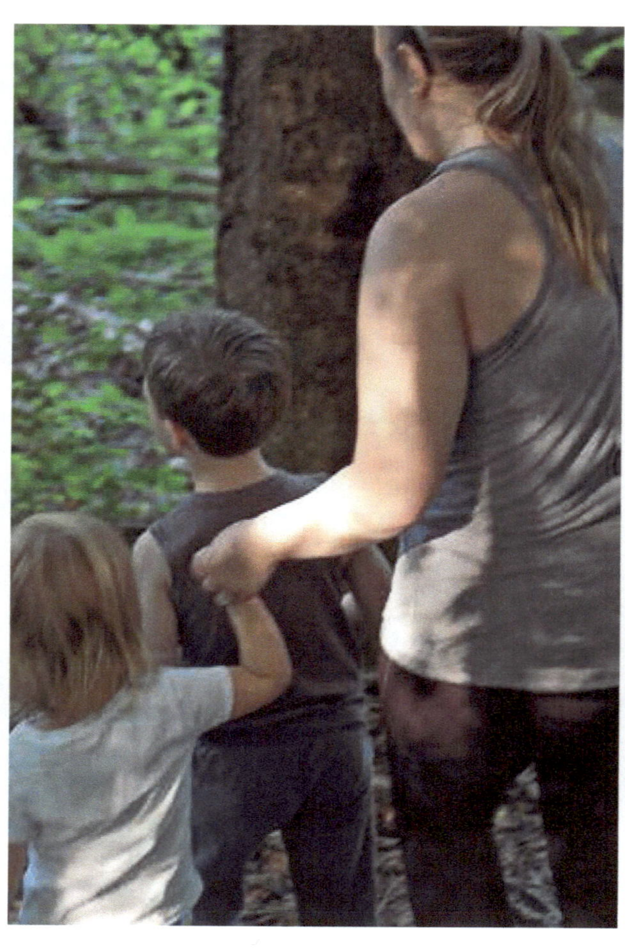 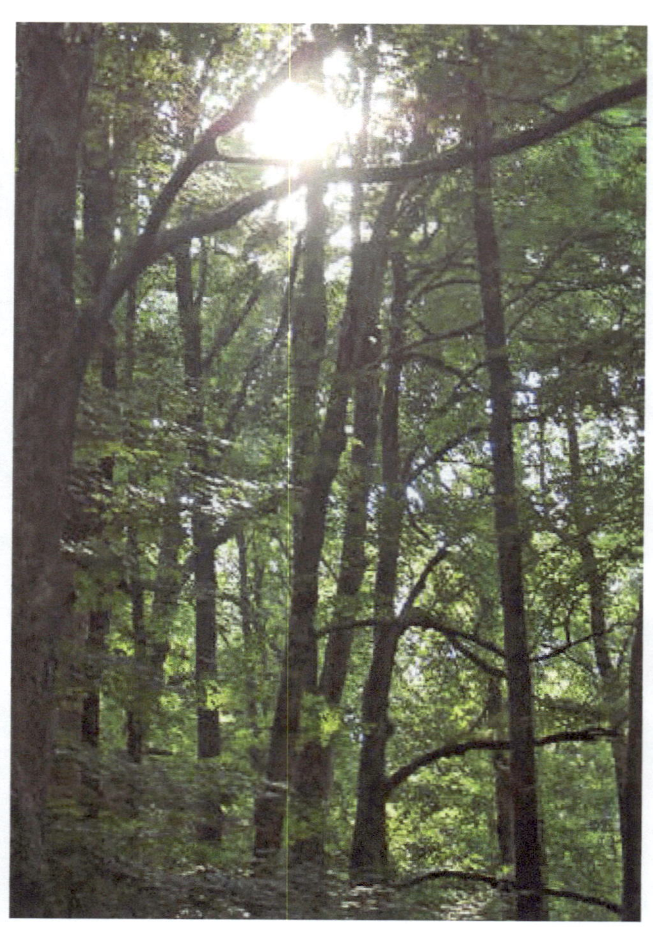

Start children off on the way they should go,
and even when they are old they will not turn from it.
PROVERBS 22:6 (NIV)

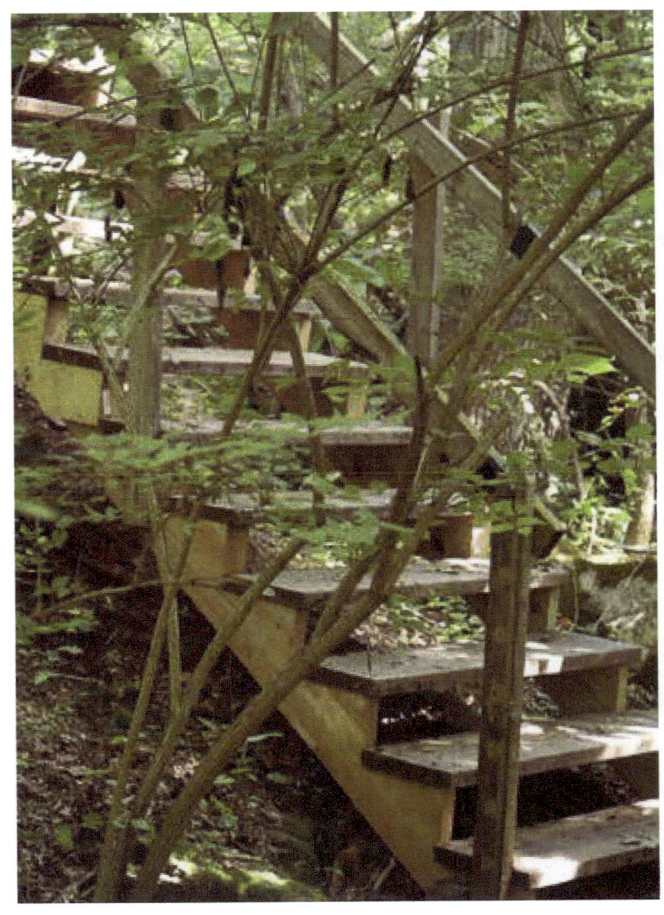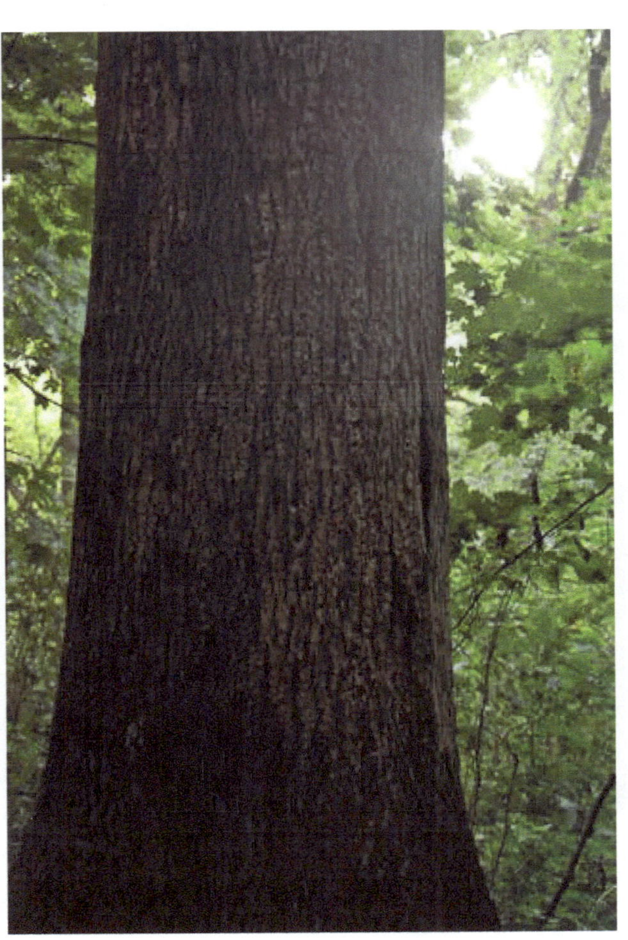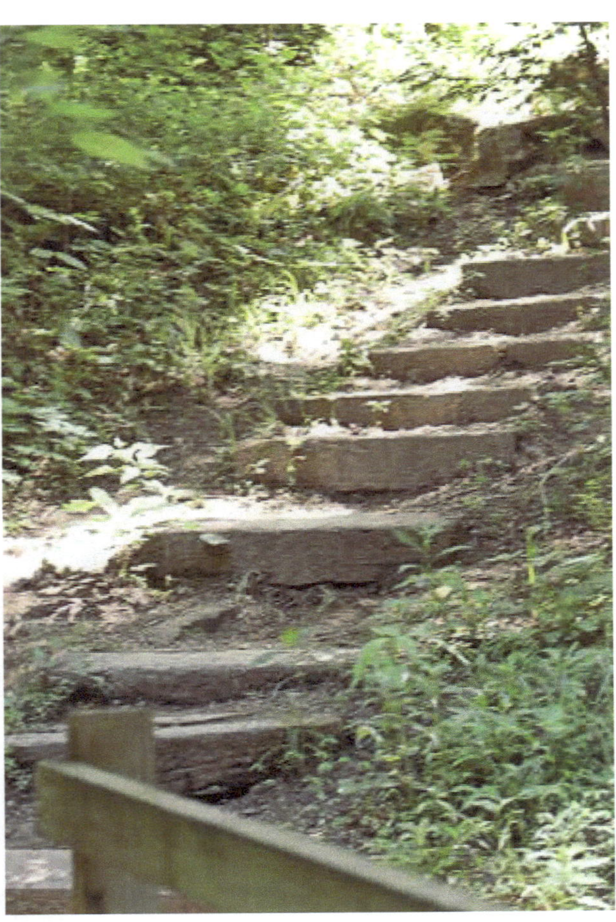

A person's steps are directed by the LORD...
PROVERBS 20:24 (NIV)

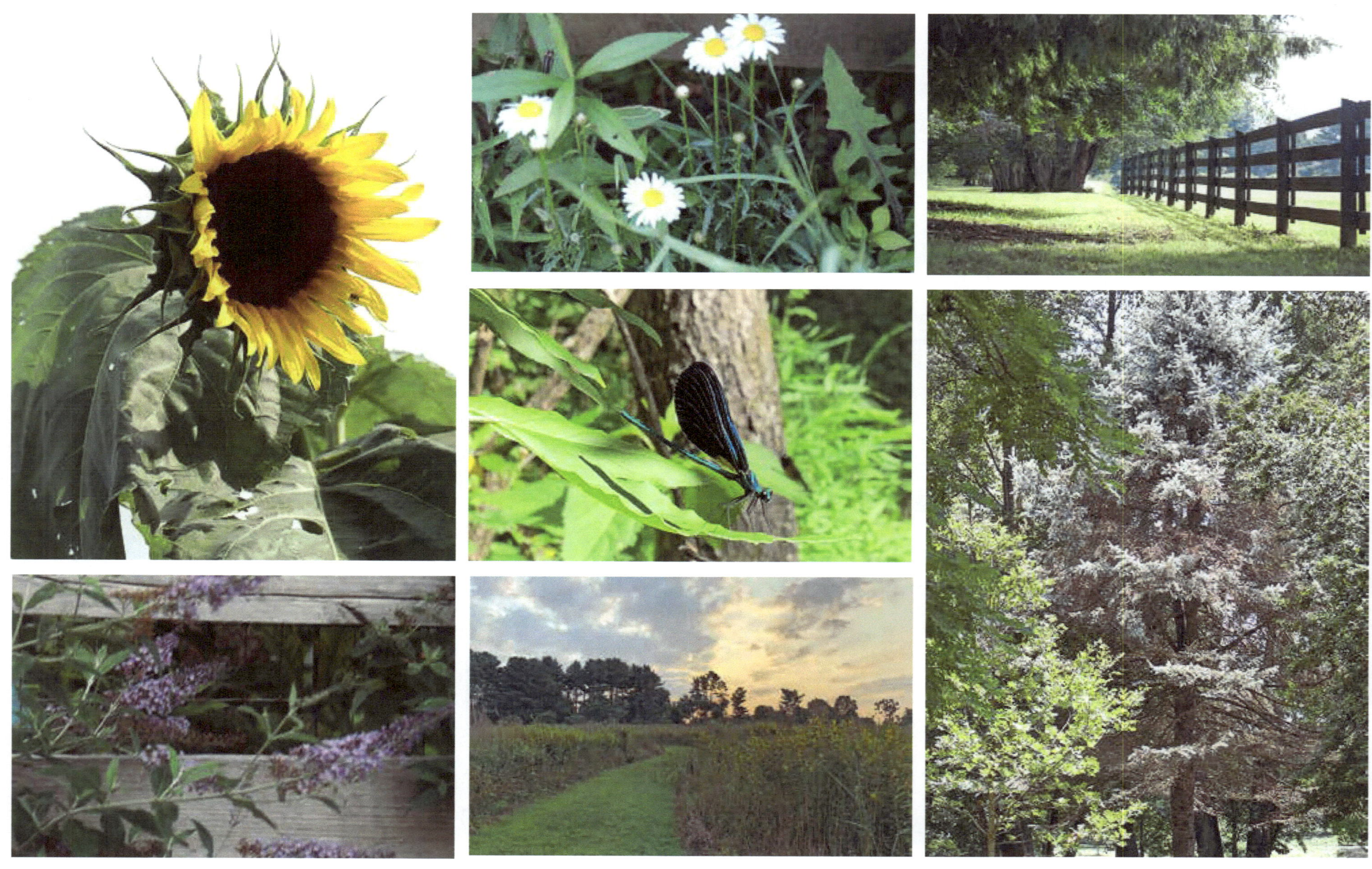

Let the fields and their crops burst out with joy!
Let the trees of the forest sing for joy before the LORD... - PSALM 96:12 (NLT)

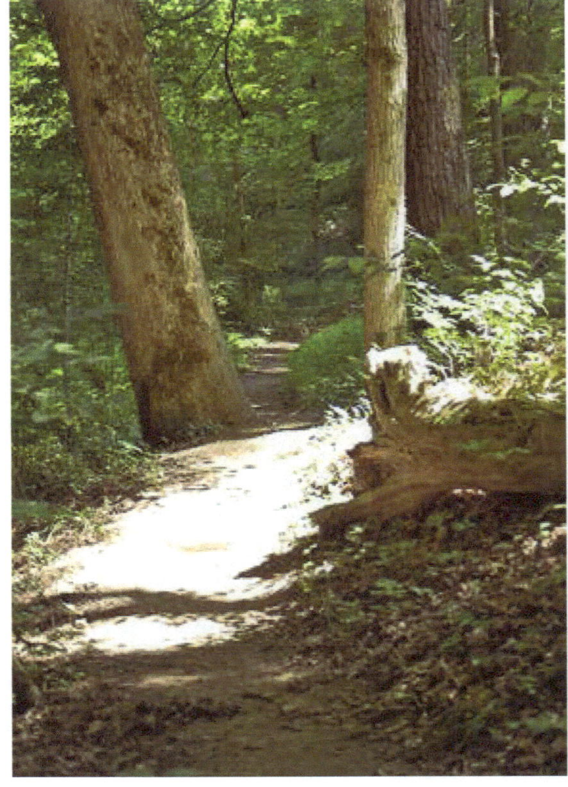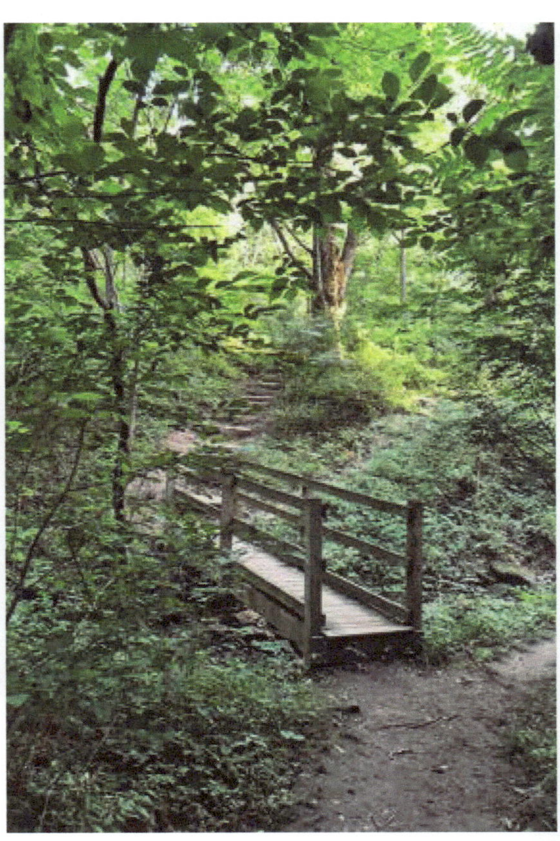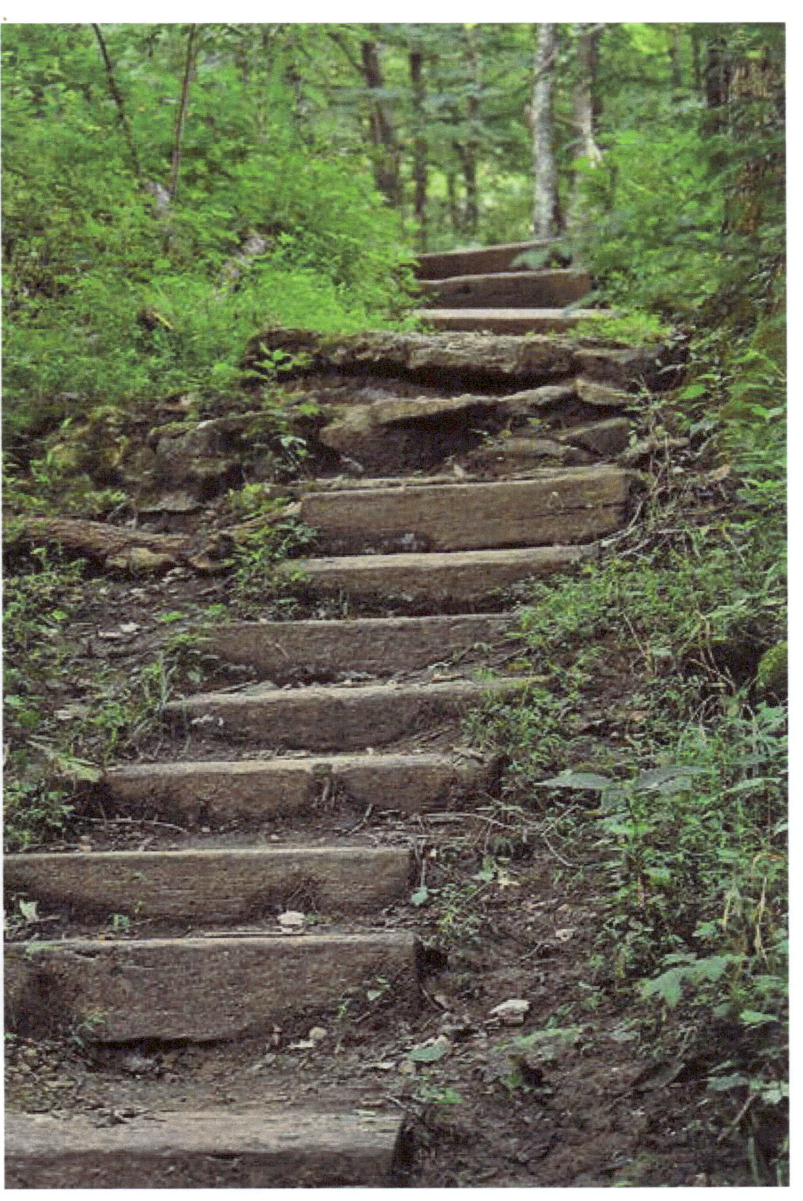

Make me walk in the path of Your commandments,
For I delight in it.
PSALM 119:35 (NASB)

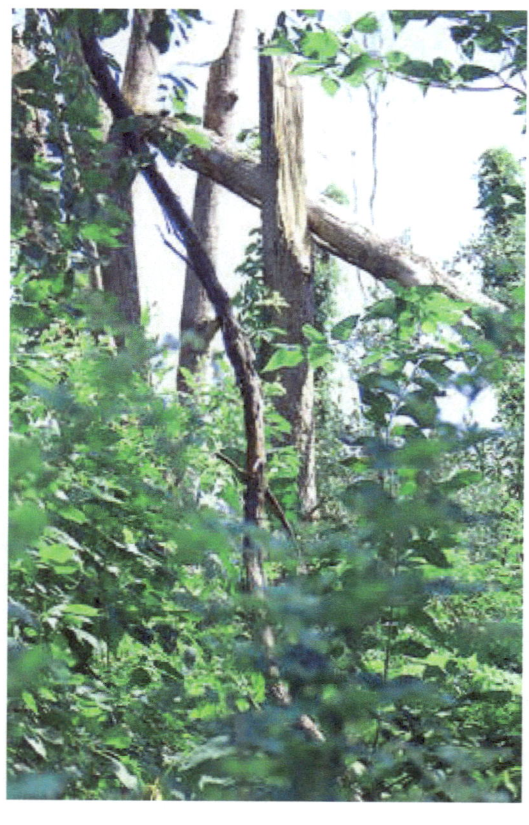

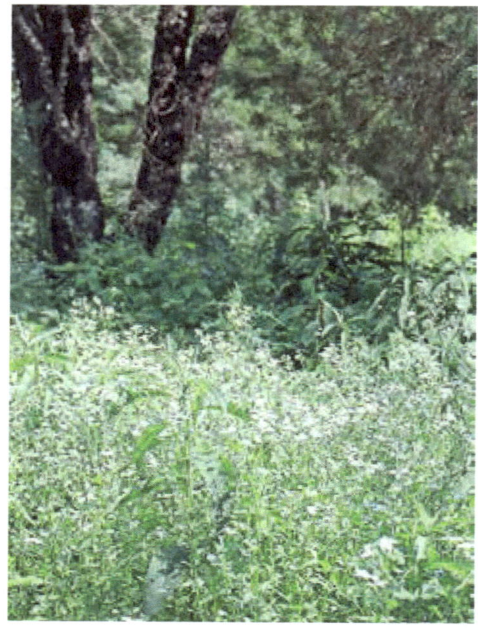

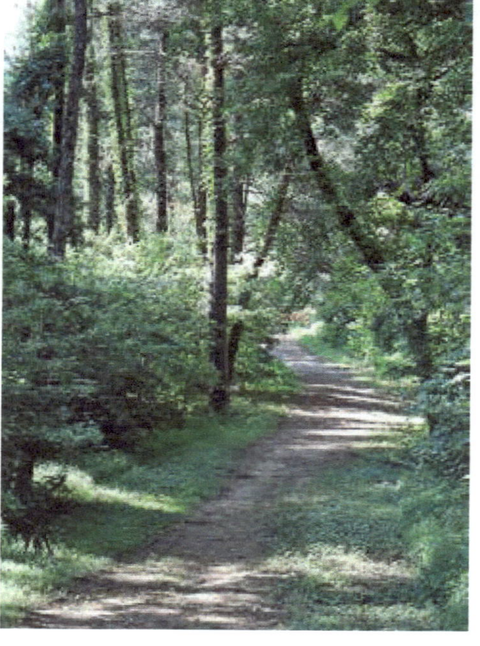

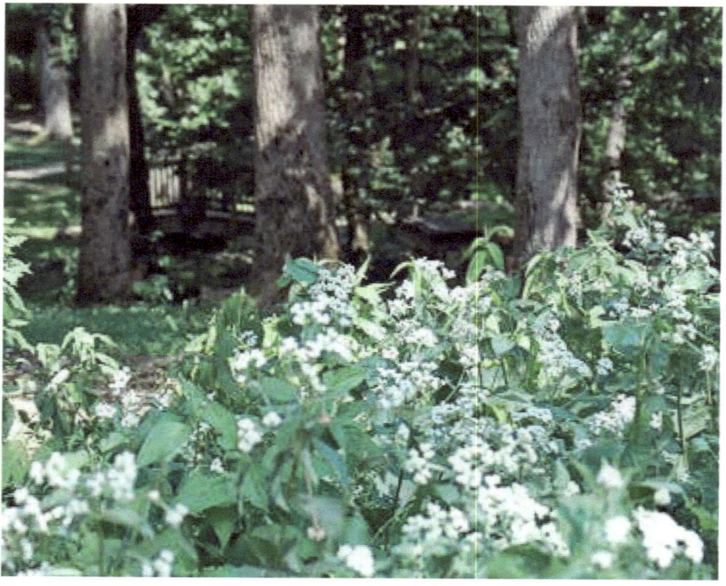

And walk in love, as Christ loved us
and gave himself up for us,
a fragrant offering and sacrifice to God.
EPHESIANS 5:2 (ESV)

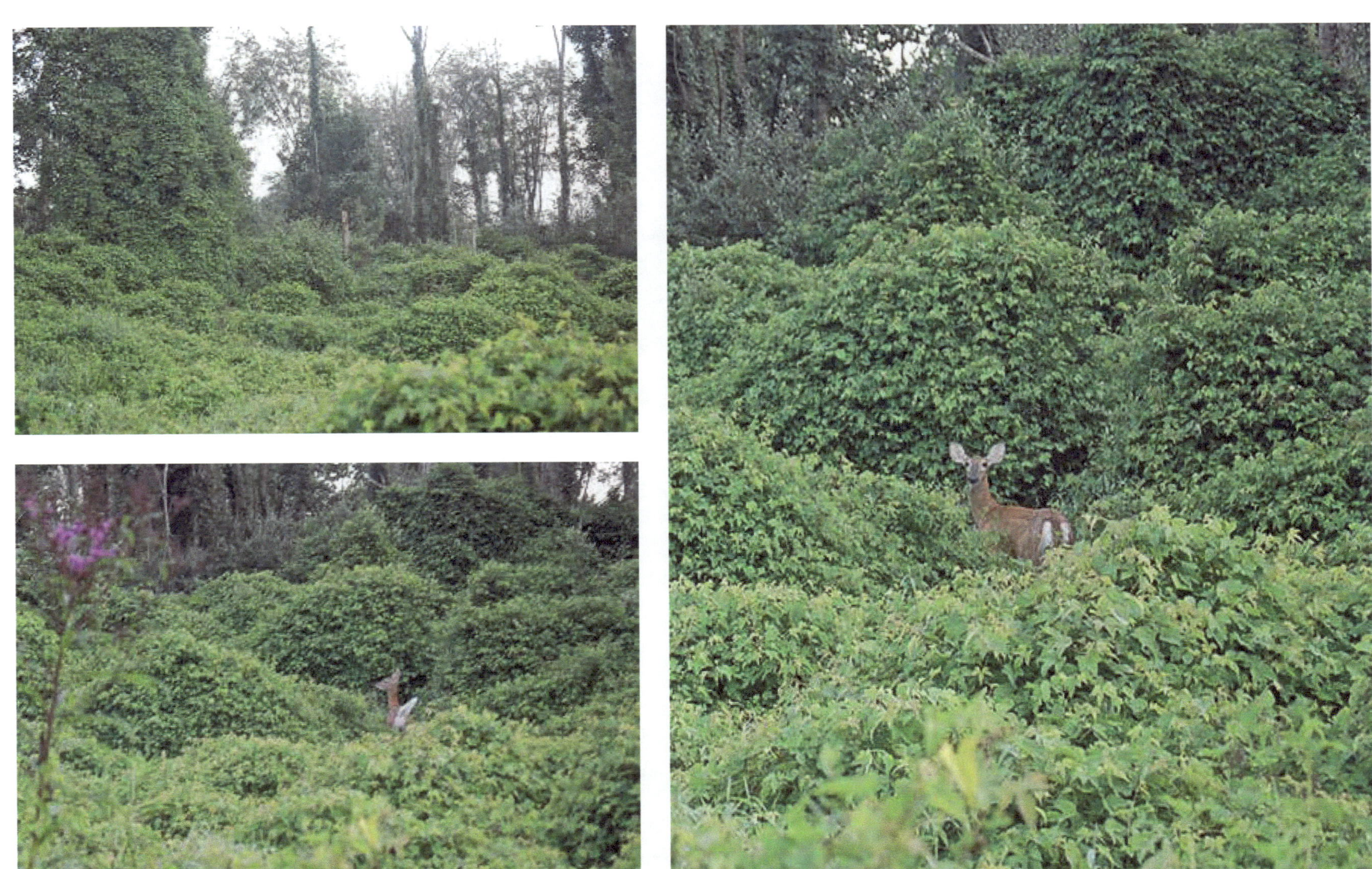

for every animal of the forest is mine...
PSALM 50:10 (NIV)

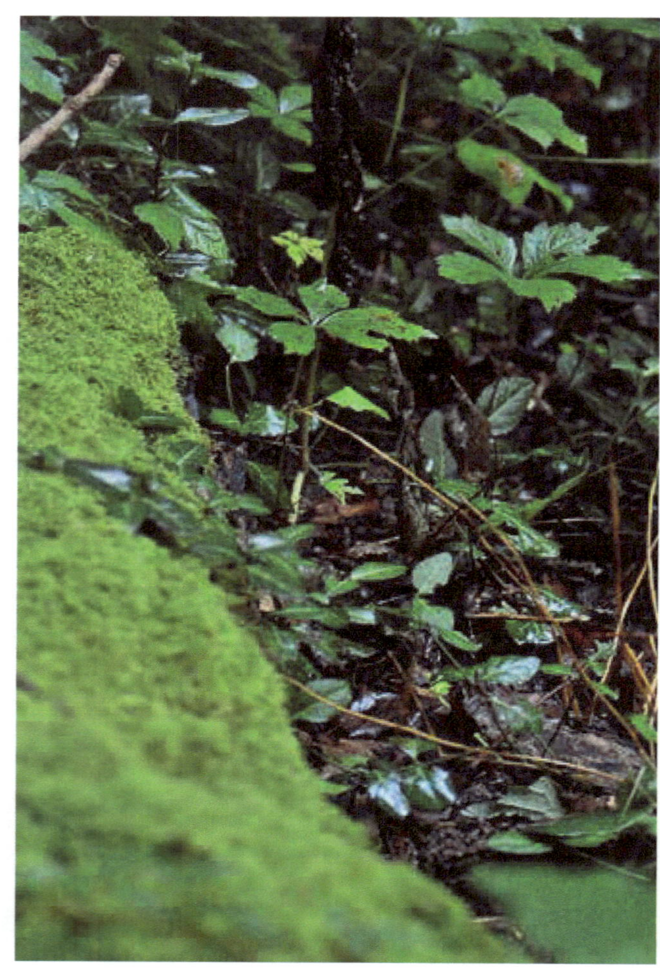

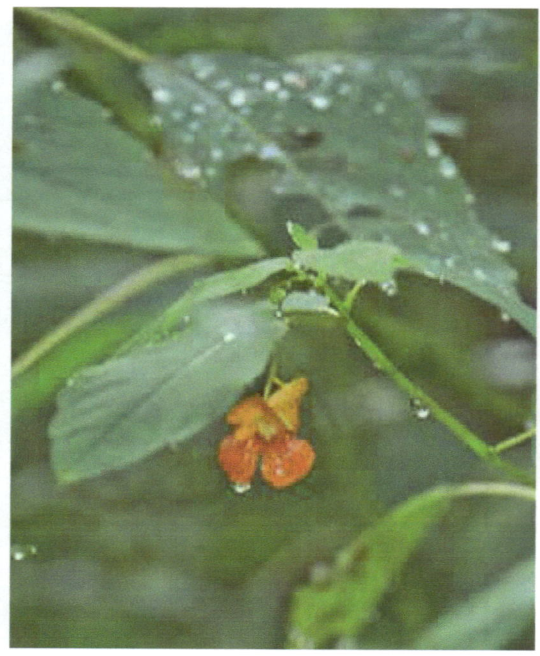

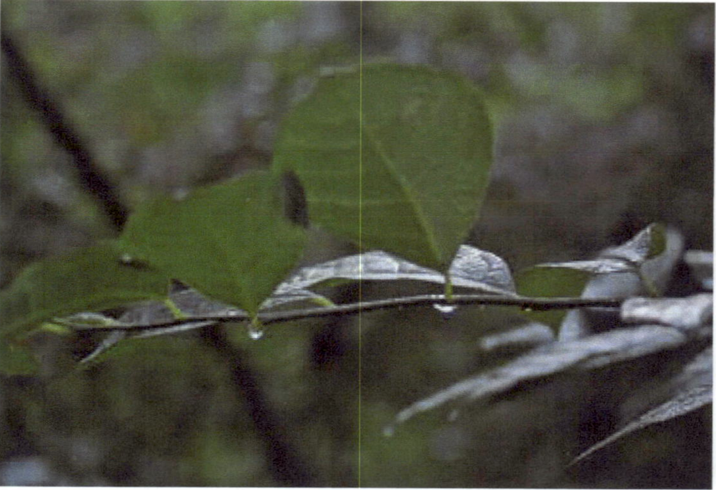

Those who sow with tears
shall reap with songs of joy!
PSALM 126:5 (ESV)

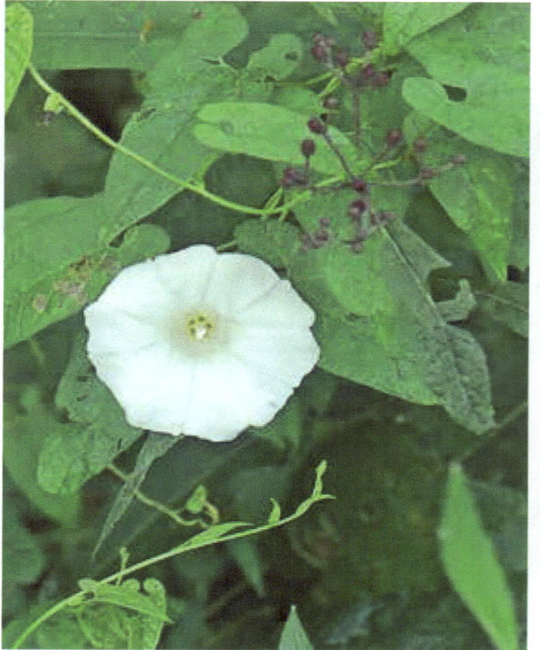

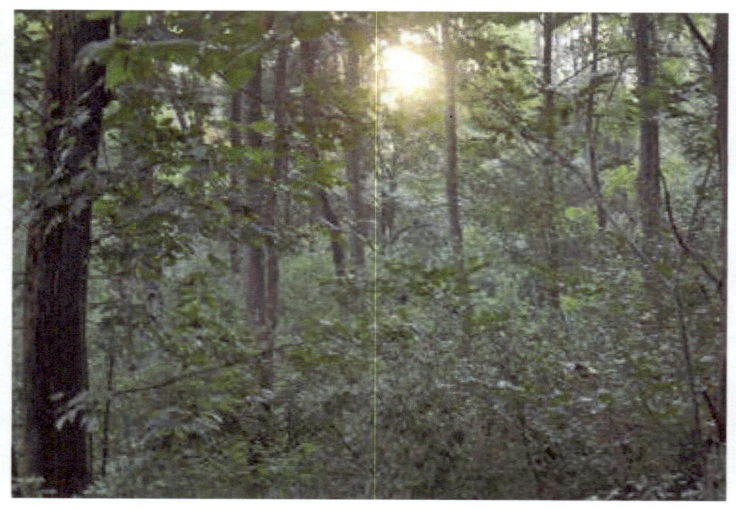

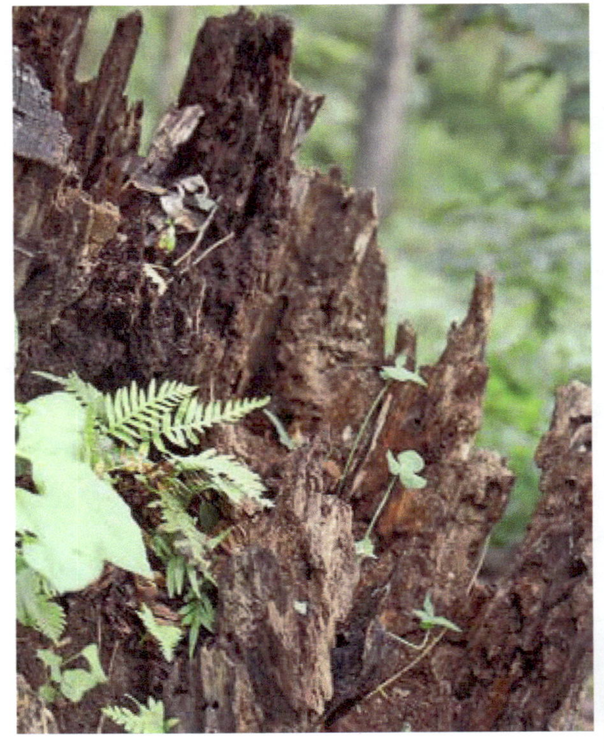
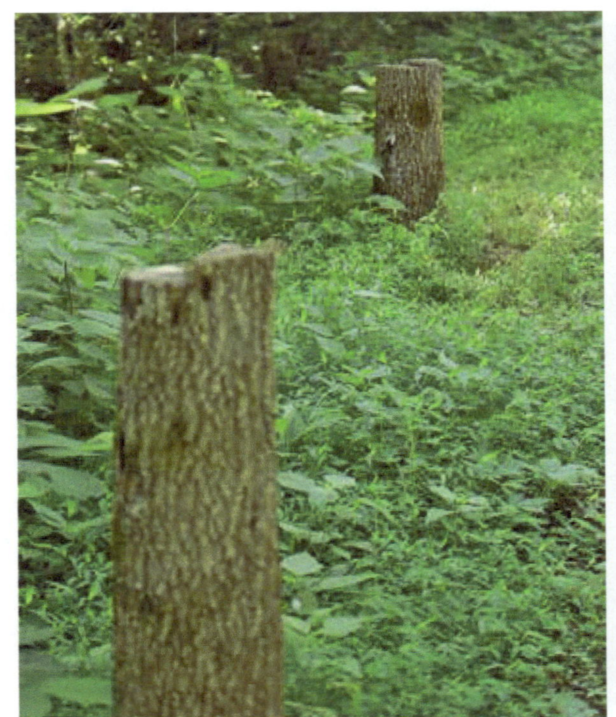
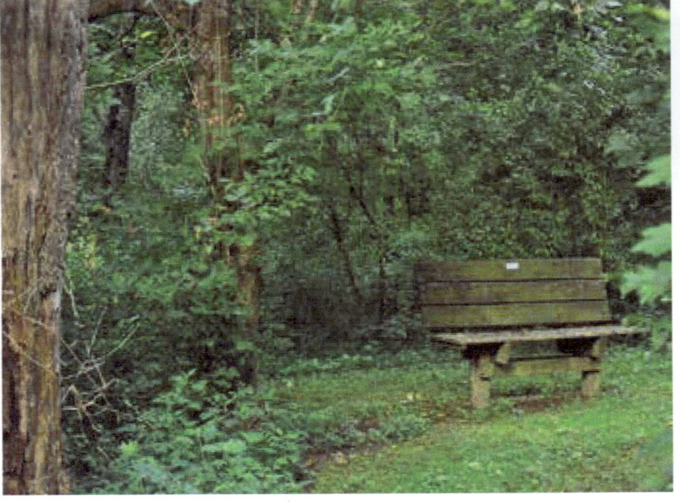
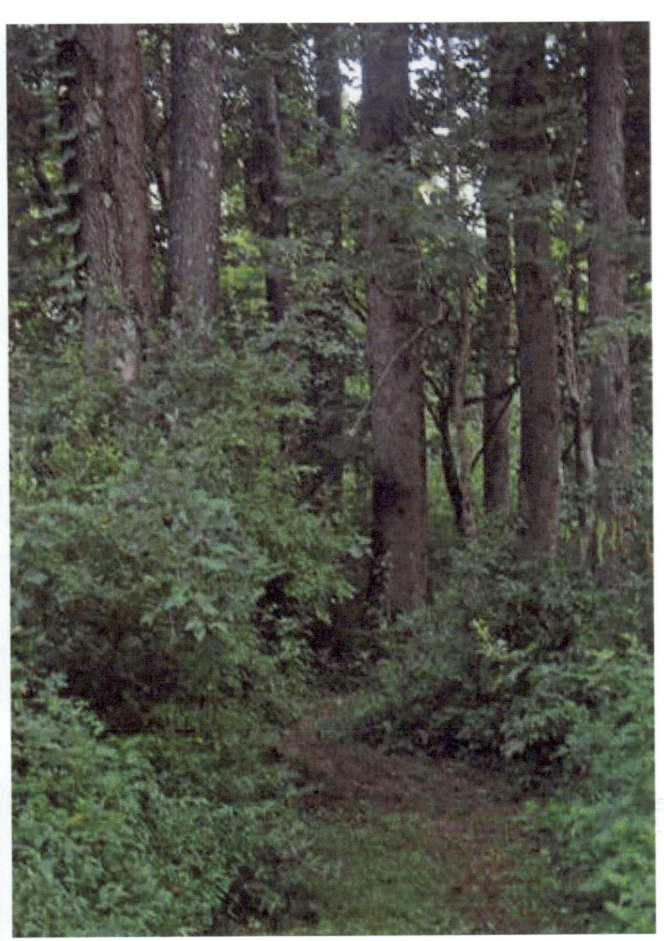

O LORD my God,
I cried out to You,
And You healed me.
PSALM 30:2 (NKJV)

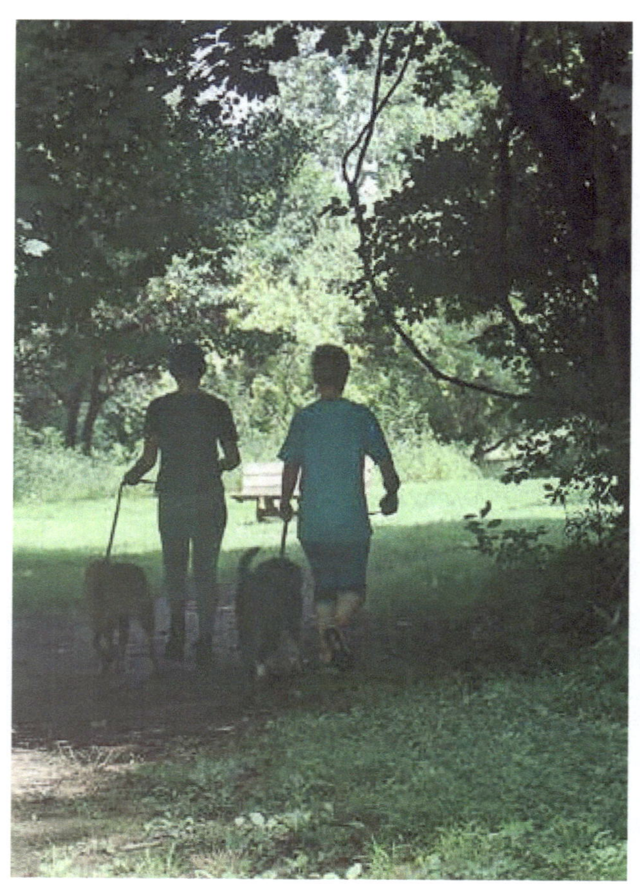 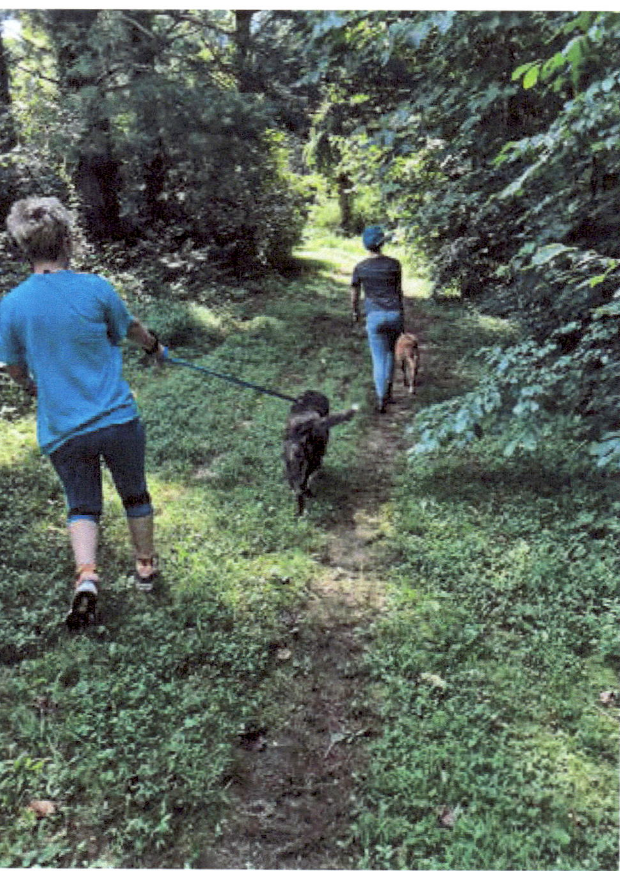 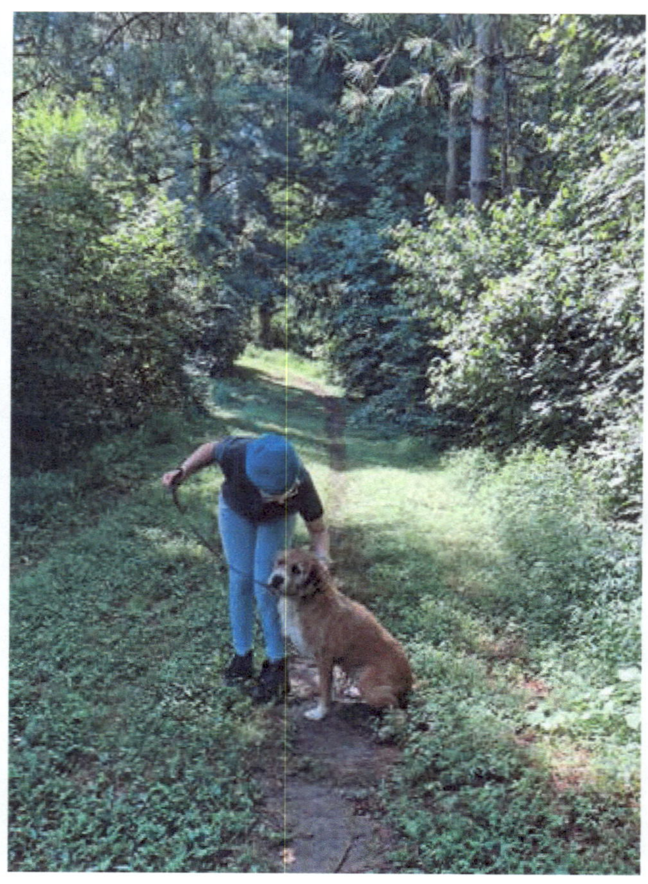

"But ask the animals, and they will teach you,
or the birds in the sky, and they will tell you...
In his hand is the life of every creature
and the breath of all mankind."
JOB 12:7-10 (NIV)

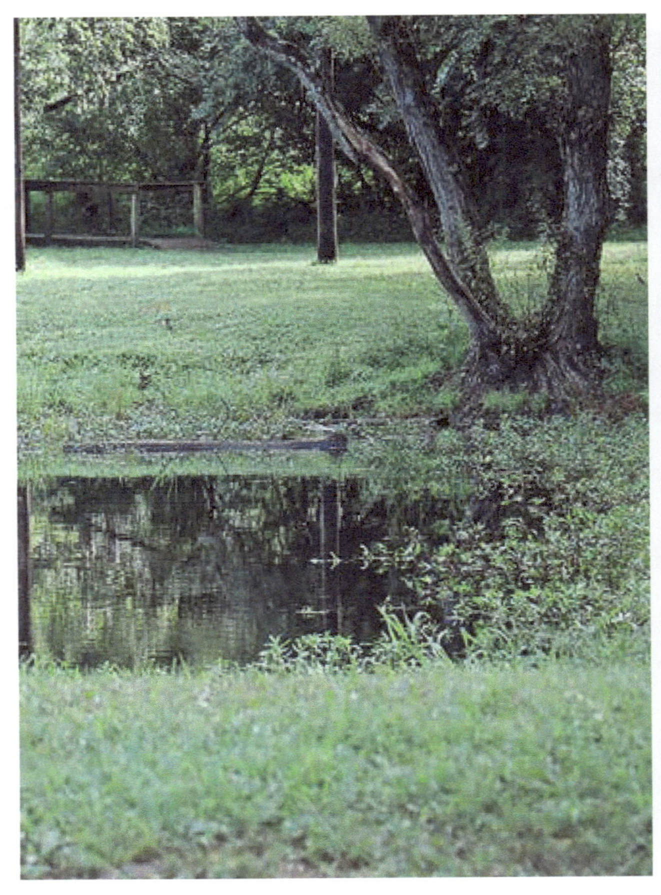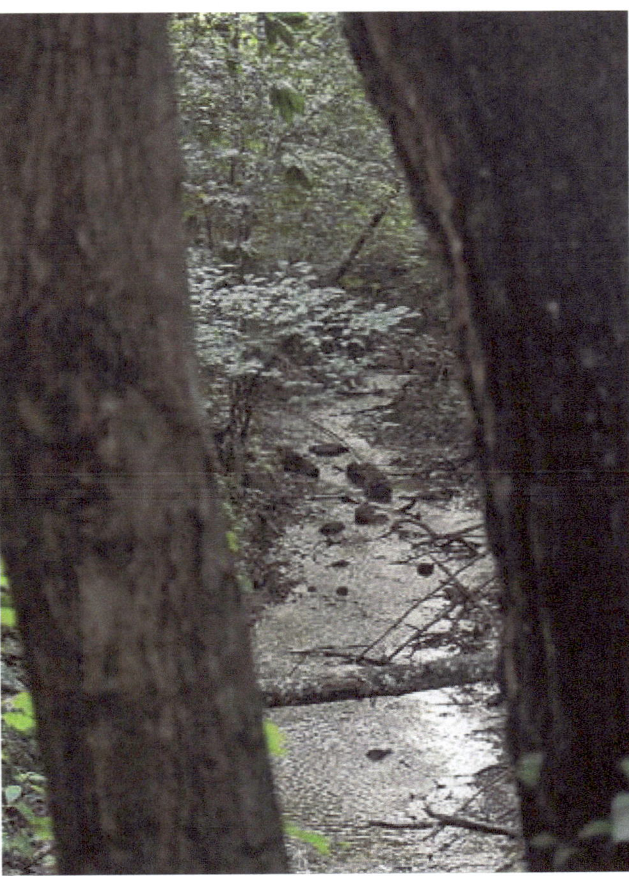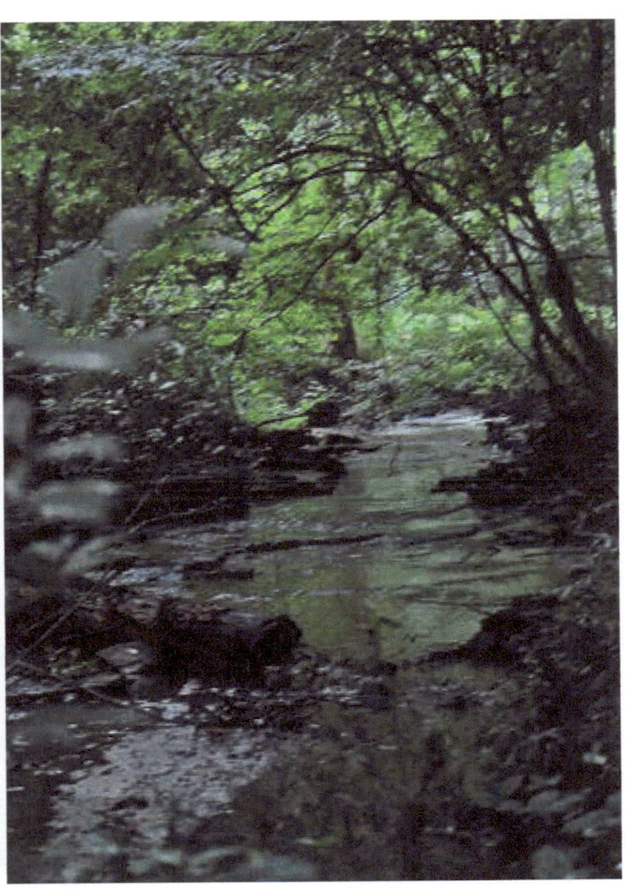

*Come,
everyone who thirsts,
come to the waters...
ISAIAH 55:1 (ESV)*

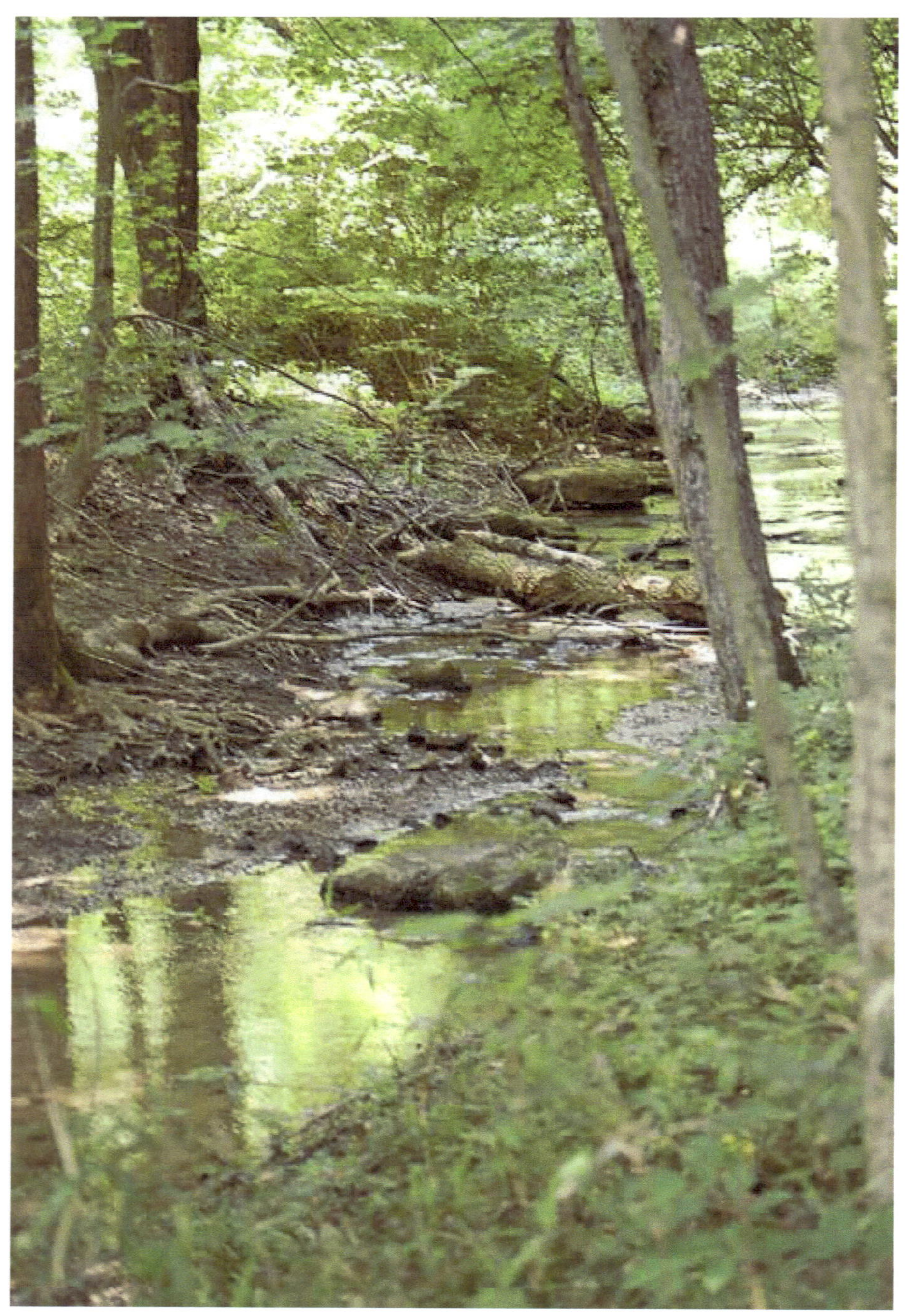

*Whoever believes in me,
as Scripture has said,
out of his heart will flow rivers of living water.*
JOHN 7:38 (NKJV)

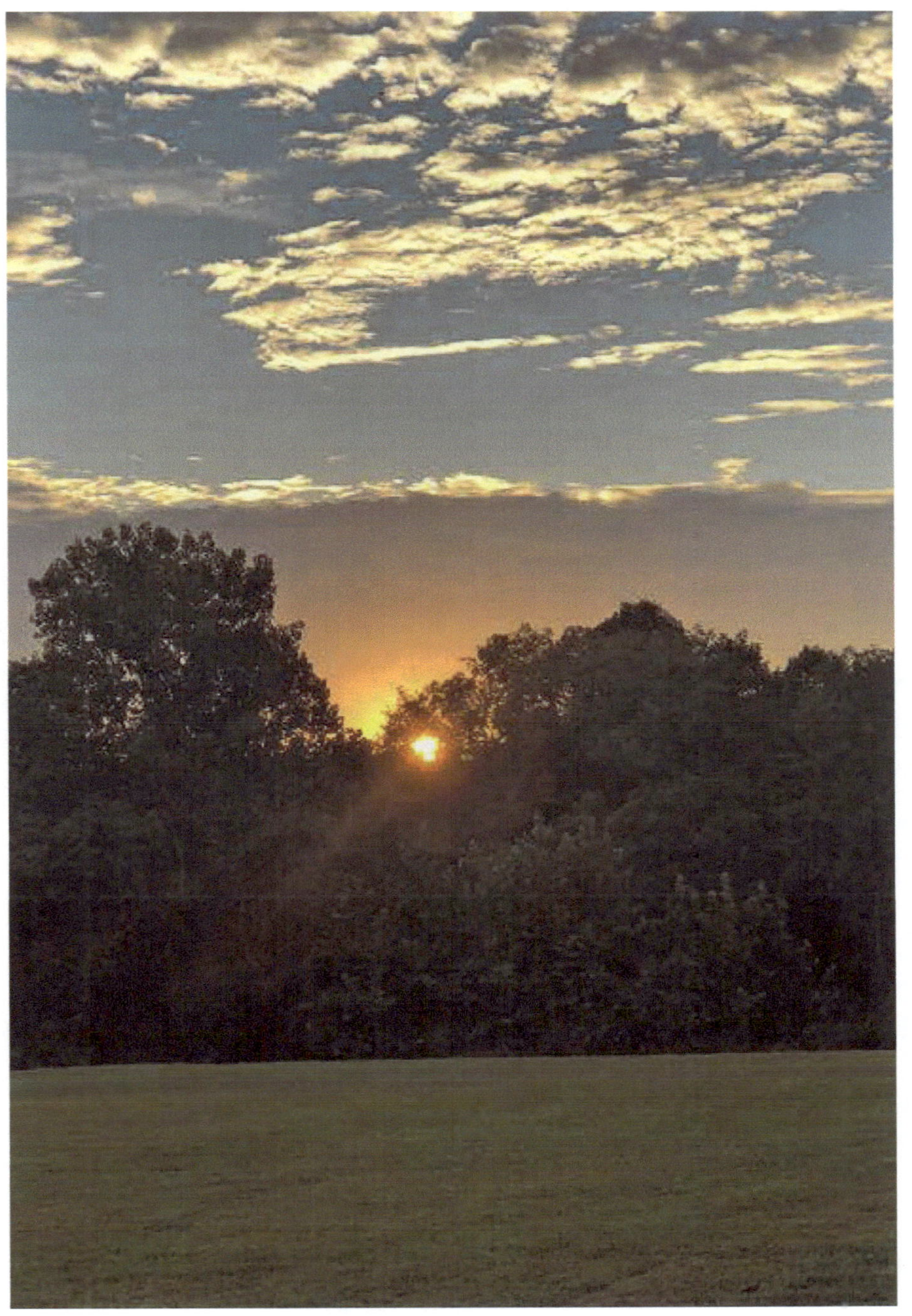

From the rising of the sun to its setting,
the name of the LORD is
to be praised.
PSALM 113:3 (NASB)

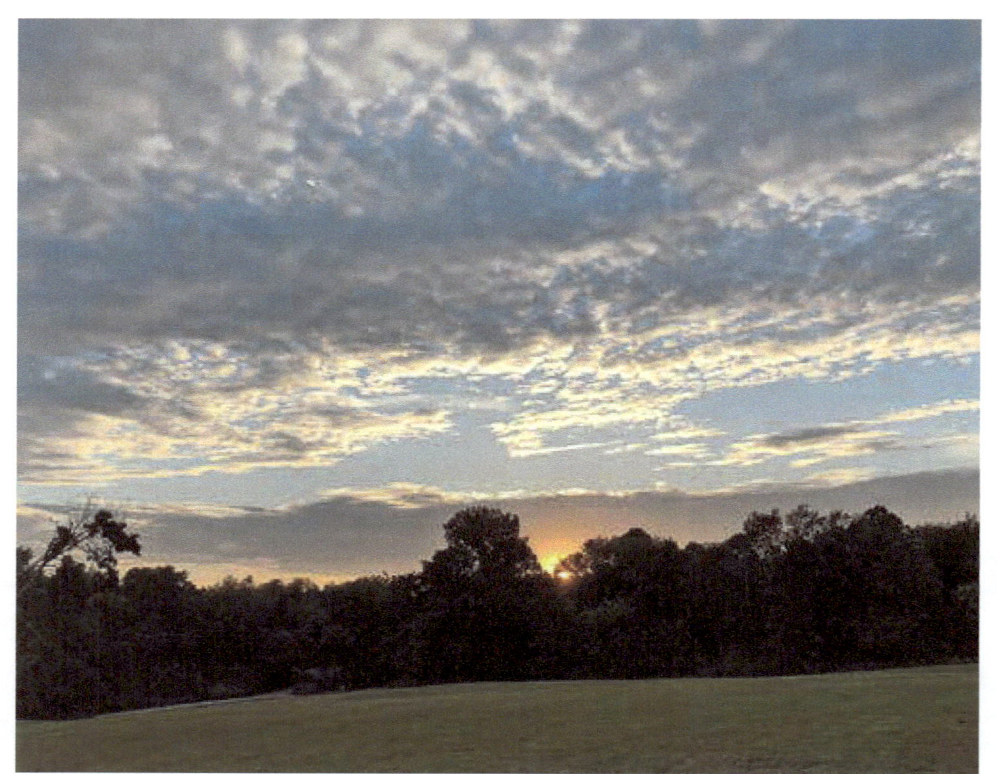 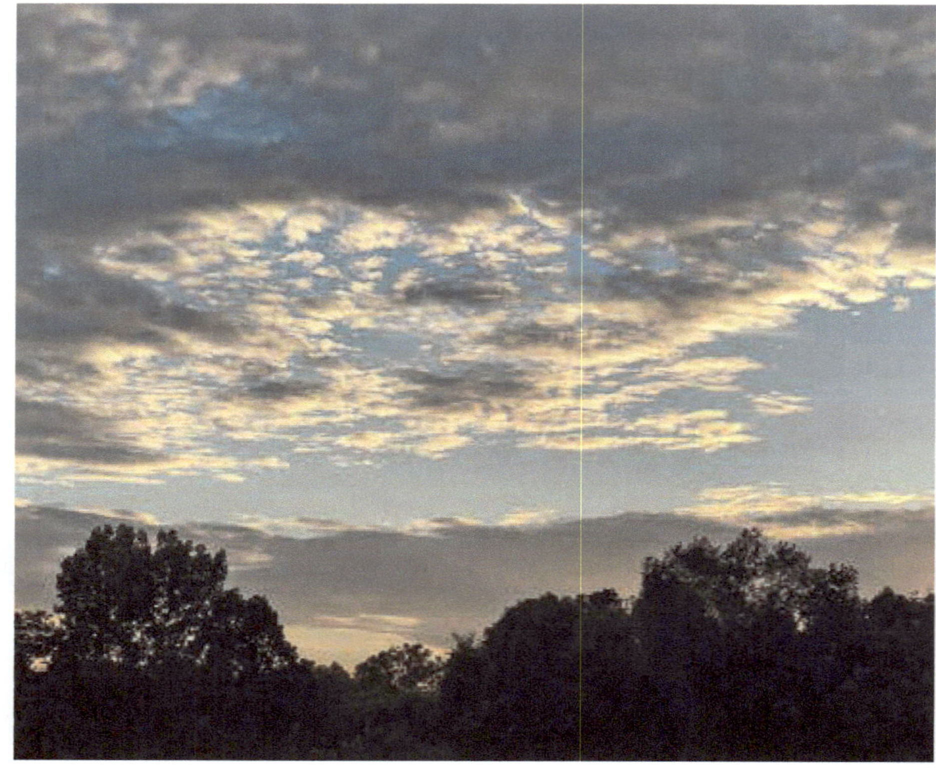

Now may the LORD of peace
himself give you peace at all times in every way. The LORD be with you all.
2 THESSALONIANS 3:16 (ESV)

ABOUT THE ACREE'S

Karin is a hard-working wife and mother of two lovely teenage daughters. Daily work and family demands are juggled with agile imperfection. To remain centered, and as time permits, she likes to cook, work out at the Y, play piano, paint (her husband Tony claims she's addicted), read, and to commune with nature--and with God--hiking through the woods.

Katy attends NOHS and is an award-winning artist. She has designed book cover artwork, logos, and painted sidewalk art in La Grange, KY. She loves photography, to write, working with young children, and singing at church.

ACKNOWLEDGEMENTS

We mindfully and prayerfully compiled this scripture photo book series of our walks through the Creasey Mahan Nature Preserve with the guidance of many family and friends. We are grateful, and blessed, by your unwavering love and support for our family. My thanks also to Tavia Brown and the wonderful staff at Creasey Mahan Nature Preserve, for your passion and dedication to conservation and transforming the Preserve into a serene outdoor sanctuary for us all to play in and enjoy.

ABOUT THE CREASEY MAHAN NATURE PRESERVE

Creasey Mahan Nature Preserve is located at 12501 Harmony Landing Road located in beautiful Goshen, Kentucky, which is approximately 30 minutes east of Louisville, Kentucky and 20 minutes west of La Grange, Kentucky. Creasey Mahan Nature Preserve is a non-profit public charity established in 1975 through the legacy of Virginia Creasey Mahan and Howard Mahan. The Nature Preserve is a 170-acre family friendly destination in Goshen that offers a complete family experience. In 2017 alone, 48,000 visitors were served through monthly events, school field trips, athletic practices and races, fun programs, and community gatherings.

The Preserve maintains three historic buildings and offers a natural history museum for educational programs. With over 9 miles of wooded trails that weave through open grasslands and four year-round springs and waterfalls, Creasey Mahan Nature Preserve is a wonderful place to relax and take a leisurely hike.

Families may enjoy using Harmony Park playground, and visit the library in the Preserve's old dairy and tobacco barn. They may also have a picnic, camp overnight, walk their dog(s), and fly a kite in one of the open grassy areas. Creasey Mahan Nature Preserve offers something for everyone!

For more information, please visit:
http://www.creaseymahannaturepreserve.org

Creasey Mahan Nature Preserve
12501 Harmony Landing Road
Goshen, Kentucky 40026
Phone: 502-228-4362
General email: Info@KYNaturepreserve.org

CREASEY MAHAN NATURE PRESERVE MAP

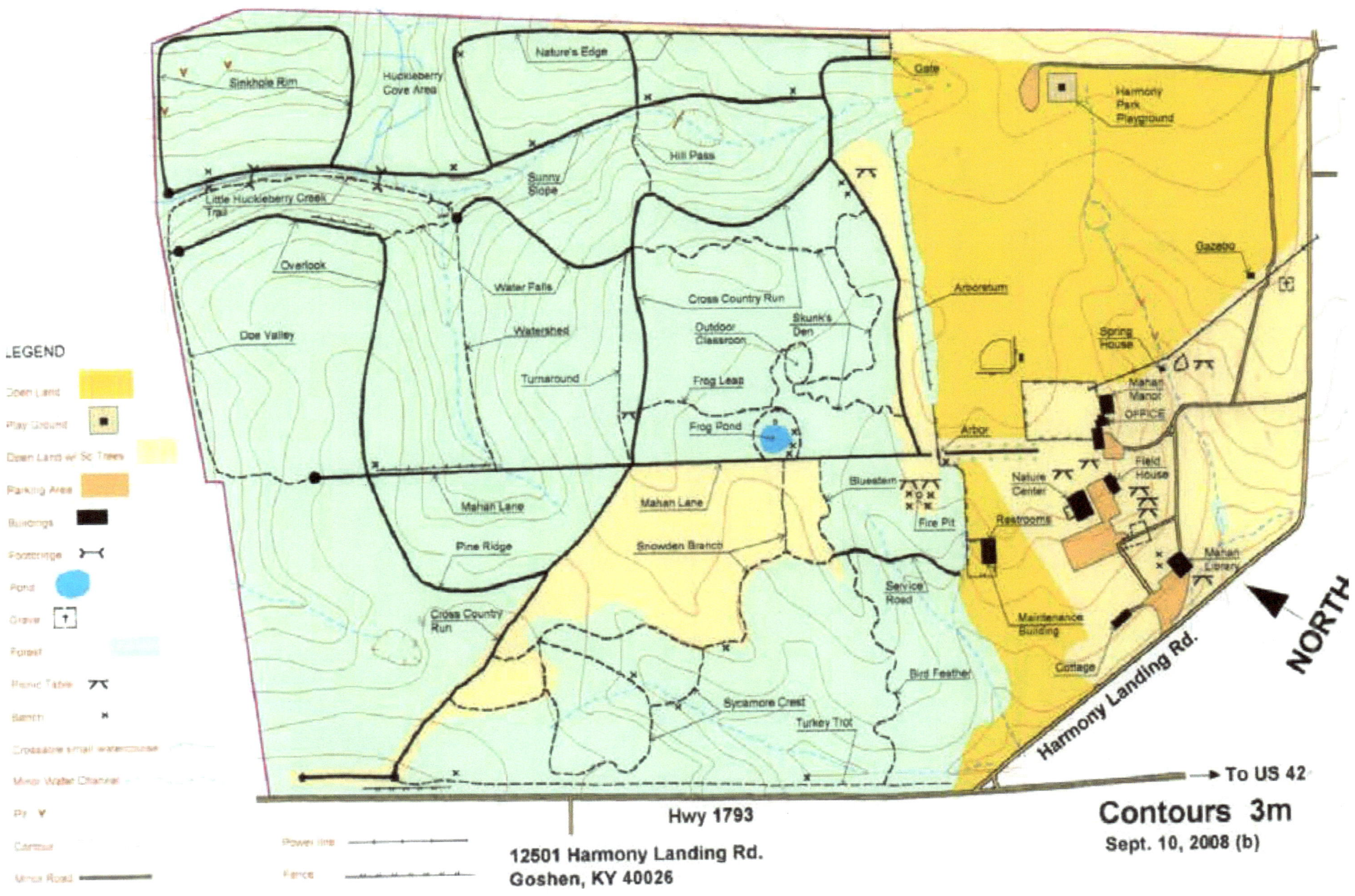

www.ingramcontent.com/pod-product-compliance
Lightning Source LLC
Chambersburg PA
CBHW040710070726

47637CB00021B/31